GRAPHIC NOVELS NOW

Building, Managing, and Marketing a Dynamic Collection

Francisca Goldsmith

American Library Association
Chicago 2005

b 28 4/21/02 4

While extensive effort has gone into ensuring the reliability of information appearing in this book, the publisher makes no warranty, express or implied, on the accuracy or reliability of the information, and does not assume and hereby disclaims any liability to any person for any loss or damage caused by errors or omissions in this publication.

Design and composition by ALA Editions in Sabon and Comic Sans using QuarkXPress 5.0 on a PC platform

Printed on 50-pound white offset, a pH-neutral stock, and bound in 10-point cover stock by McNaughton & Gunn

The paper used in this publication meets the minimum requirements of American National Standard for Information Sciences—Permanence of Paper for Printed Library Materials, ANSI Z39.48-1992. ∞

Library of Congress Cataloging-in-Publication Data

Goldsmith, Francisca.
   Graphic novels now : building, managing, and marketing a dynamic collection / Francisca Goldsmith.
      p. cm.
   Includes bibliographical references and index.
   ISBN 0-8389-0904-3 (alk. paper)
   1. Libraries—Special collections—Graphic novels. 2. Graphic novels—United States. I. Title.
   Z692.G7G65 2005
   025.2'77415973—dc22   2005012653

Printed in the United States of America

09 08 07 06 05   5 4 3 2 1

Z
692
.G7
G65
2005

CONTENTS

Although the first pair of chapters deal at length and in detail with the conceptual and practical aspects of defining the graphic novel, let me say up front and straightaway that the concern of this book is limited to fully extended literary works published in a medium that combines text and image to present a narrative. I am not including single-joke or single-idea comics—even if brought together into an anthology—or comics serials derived from syndicated characters in the realm I am admittedly defining narrowly.

Rather than taking a broad view of what some might call graphic novels, I am instead taking a broad view of the place and the role graphic novels have in contemporary libraries and for contemporary readers. Where libraries have placed all comics-oriented print under the rubric of graphic novel, the discussions, suggestions, and questions posed in this book can be extended to include anthologies and syndicated series. In fact, however, this book is limited to discussing monographs that present their stories—whether fiction or nonfiction—in a format requiring the reader to take both image and word into consideration and to work between them to create his or her understanding and enjoyment of the creator's (or creators') work.

I have read comics all my life, but I have my own personal taste limitations. (I have also read murder mysteries most of my life and am influenced by a set of taste limitations there as well). My professional hope for comics—especially for fully extended graphic novels—is that libraries come to normalize them. Graphic novels are books, they have writers, they have readers. The content and subject matter of graphic novels and the critical abilities and ages of those involved with them are no less diverse than the same attributes as they attach to film: some are serious, some created from the soul, some of more interest to older adults than to any other demographic . . . while others—but you get the point.

Yes, American teens like graphic novels, but in American libraries, graphic novels are at risk for being seen as suiting only a specific age, just as board books are usually relegated to a certain part of the library and assumed to appeal only to specific users or potential users. I hope that this book moves the many wonderful discussions so many young adult librarians have been having over the past ten years into a bibliographic arena that is wide enough to let graphic novels find, and be found by, every possible demographic any library might serve.

ACKNOWLEDGMENTS

It was due to my good fortune in finding a job as a young adult librarian that I was able to develop my voice as a proponent of graphic novels in libraries. Without the discussions my profession made possible with the likes of Art Spiegelman, Will Eisner, Jessica Abel, Steve Raiteri, Kat Kan, Michele Gorman, David Serchay, Libby Flynn, Charles Brownstein, and, of course, Rory Root, I would have a lot of personal opinions but no portfolio. Steve Miller's Graphic Novels in Libraries List (GNLIB-L) has been a constant source of food for thought. (For detailed information about the history of, archives to, and current mailing list procedures for GNLIB-L, hosted by Topica, see http://www.angelfire.com/comics/gnlib/index.html.) Mike Pawuk generously invited me to serve on the preconference committee that brought the Young Adult Library Services Association (YALSA) its highly successful "Getting Graphic @ your library" preconference in 2002. Thank you, all, for including me as the ideas whipped around rooms, over the e-mail transom, and in planes and vans—not to mention in the back hallways and front lobbies of various libraries.

Thanks to Dean Linnard, the almost-fifteen-year-old artist to whom I knew I could turn when it became clear that chapter 2 needed image as well as word.

And of course the fact that Bob Saunderson continues to let me litter our household with graphic novels at every stage, from galleys to molting former favorites, requires acknowledgment and gratitude. Thanks last, but he knows not least, to Fred Saunderson, who consorts with me to paper the house in comics but who also makes dinner when his mother forgets to stop reading.

CHAPTER 1

Why Graphic Novels Now?

Modern Readers, Modern Libraries

The day in 1986 that cartoonist Art Spiegelman's previously serialized story of his father's Holocaust survival was released in book format, I purchased a copy for myself on the way home from work. Although the West Coast university library where I was then employed regularly purchased history, art, and literature titles—and although I had been aware of the impending publication of *Maus: A Survivor's Tale* in book format—my coworkers deemed my interest in it peculiar at best, intellectually aberrant at worst. The term *graphic novel* was not familiar to many outside of publishing. Graphic novels looked like comics, and most librarians did not admit to reading or thinking about comics—except in those special archives far away in the Midwest. Less than two decades ago, most American libraries knew exactly two things about comics: (1) comics did not belong in libraries because they were not real books and (2) nobody with any intellectual sense (that is, the library's perceived user) reads them anyway.

In 1989, I changed jobs. At my new library, a small, urban, public system that prided itself on being the busiest per capita in the state, I was pleased to find *Maus* within the collection. What I found arguable, however, was that it had been relegated to the art collection, classified simply as a comic strip album. Although it was easy enough for me to convince fellow public service librarians that the title in question might be better suited to a Dewey home where readers of history, Judaica, or biography

1

would be able to find it readily, the technical services staff seemed dubious. Reluctantly, however, they made the classification change.

That battle won, I naively went comic book shopping for my new primary responsibility, a young adult collection that was then in a neonatal state. This time, however, the cataloger who had let me win the case for *Maus*'s placement in the adult collection wasn't going to let any more of these troublesome comics confuse the flow of materials through technical services. The lot was returned summarily to me, with a note suggesting I shelve them uncataloged. However, one exception was made: Scott Hampton's adaptation of Robert E. Howard's horror story, *Pigeons from Hell*, which the technical services supervisor declared to be too strange for public consumption, was locked into the bottom drawer of his desk, where it was unearthed a year later by his successor. In the meantime, I had found and read *Comics Librarianship: A Handbook*, by archivist Randall Scott and public library cataloger Sandy Berman.[1] Though that book concerned cataloging comic books as serials and maintaining collections as collectibles, it gave me the technical services vocabulary I needed to start a conversation about making graphic novels publicly accessible in our library. By the time reference resource editor D. Aviva Rothschild published *Graphic Novels: A Bibliographic Guide to Book-Length Comics*, thus offering collection developers critical annotations for hundreds of graphic novels and comics compilations, my library had become a kind of demonstration model, connecting readers, graphic novels, and professional librarians across service lines.[2] *Pigeons from Hell* had been released from the drawer and cataloged, and was rarely shelved due to its continual circulation, which wore out several copies. Now with a technical services ally and a public user group that expected to be able to find graphic novels at the library, I worked to identify and address the plethora of professional concerns and issues related to collecting, processing, circulating, and promoting such materials.

Timing can mean a lot in a project like this one. Certainly my own situation was not unique because in the past decade libraries and librarians, comics creators and publishers, booksellers and readers have worked to promote professional understanding and standards of inclusion on one another's behalf. Graphic novels raise many of the classic library science issues: To what, exactly, does the term apply? How can an item of this type be described bibliographically? How does a selector determine which item of this format belongs in the collection for which potential readers? Who are the potential readers? How can items in this format be readied for circulation and stored in a manner that allows the would-be reader to obtain them? How can they be marketed to an audience wider than those already in the know? Where does the graphic novel fit in the universe of intellectual and aesthetic exploration that libraries support? Where can the local library staff turn for professional assistance with thorny questions about classification, processing, or challenges to specific titles?

In 2002, the Young Adult Library Services Association (YALSA) sponsored a preconference at the American Library Association's Annual Conference that brought librarians from diverse institutional types together to explore, celebrate, and analyze the fit between graphic novels and library services. In one session at this "Getting Graphic @ your library" preconference, I expected to facilitate a discussion among no more than a dozen or so attendees on the topic of graphic novels and bibliographic control. To my immense surprise, the room filled to capacity—about seventy-five folks. Public young adult librarians, private school librarians, prison librarians, vendors, and even library directors—staff from both coasts and everywhere in the middle of the country—turned out to ask about reading habits, suggest practical shelving methods, debate classification schemes, and plead for guidance in formulating budgets for graphic novels. Discussions among participants yielded many good suggestions for addressing various details of bibliographic control, and a few excellent examples of what was working well in various parts of libraryland emerged. What happened in that room that day was the beginning of an articulation of the issues, some prescriptive steps, and methods for planning both the execution and the documentation of best practices.

This guide grows directly from those experiences. My intent is to provide enough information for you to feel comfortable tackling any and all of the questions listed above. If you have never read a graphic novel, or have only glanced at a page or two in those passing through your work area, this guide will not substitute for the kind of firsthand experience you will need to provide adequate evaluations, book talks, or programs centered on graphic novels. On the other hand, if you already feel acquainted with the format, this guide can help you to organize and crystallize your understanding and appreciation in ways that help you to communicate with other library staff about graphic novels, to write professional reviews that boost the amount of critical information available to libraries about graphic novels, to include graphic novels in your readers' advisory efforts, and to develop programs that expand your community's familiarity with both graphic novels and your library's array of literary and service options.

I intentionally omitted questions that begin with *why* from the list above: Why graphic novels? Why consider their place in libraries? Why now? To place the topic in context, we will start with those *why* questions. History is a great lamp to use when exploring why a situation exists in the present. We will use a three-bulb lamp to illuminate the diverse aspects of the past that inform the current need to bring graphic novels and libraries together systematically.

TODAY'S LIBRARY

Once upon a time, libraries collected scrolls and, later, incunabula. The centuries rolled by and the technologies for recording human intellectual experience, as well as the intellectual experiences themselves, changed. And libraries—as well as their maintainers and their users—changed and continue to change. Library staff both organize aspects of intellectual culture so that they are retrievable and comprehendible by the current generation and lay out methods of access to history, imagination, and contemporary culture for generations to come. The library is both a storehouse (sometimes concrete, sometimes virtual) and a forum for activities related to the exchange of ideas. As such, it retains the past, corroborates and challenges the present, and provides formal guidance toward the future.

In the library, intellectual, organizational, and access matters are not solved once and for all. Instead, they are resolved, reconsidered, and readied for what happens next, even while documenting what has happened up to now. Methods for coping with new technologies, emerging political and social norms, and user groups that change with exposure to the new need ongoing reassessment, adjustment, and clarification.

Although it is time to look at how libraries can plan their treatment of graphic novels and to examine the library science issues related to including those materials in our ancient institution, it should be noted that much of the discussion must happen in the future. The considerations, approaches, and suggestions in this book reflect the fact that graphic novels are already here—created and published just like other books, and then collected and read through libraries and distributed through other consumer channels. But we must also realize that, given the newness of the form and its even newer recognition by libraries, the discussion of best practices is only beginning.

Libraries are one part—and not even half—of the equation that states our need to identify and plan so that people have access to graphic novels through our bibliocentric institutions. To address the whys of graphic novel librarianship, we need to clarify the term *graphic novel* itself and then consider what makes contemporary readers appreciate and understand what graphic novels do and how they do it.

FROM CARICATURE TO GRAPHIC NOVEL: A QUICK HISTORY

Where did graphic novels come from? How have their creators and consumers developed the fact of this form?

Although both scholars and pundits have asserted that comics are descended from cave art or the Bayeux Tapestry, a more compelling case can be made for tracing them back at least to the European master painters of the sixteenth to eighteenth centuries who developed the elements of caricature.[3] Fantastic features and exaggerated gestures in the works of Bosch and Goya communicate both feeling and allegorical message. Rather than idealizing or providing a realistic reflection, caricature communicates insidiously. Technological inventions inspired artists such as William Hogarth (1697–1764) to render images that could be shared more broadly than works that were drawn or painted individually. Hogarth's satiric lithographs include a set of four caricatures depicting the course of activities in Parliament on one day. *The Election* (1754) thus recounts a narrative through sequential art.[4]

By the early nineteenth century, caricature had become a formal satirical act and its appreciation spawned periodicals dedicated to its showcase. Honoré Daumier (1808–1879) used caricature to suggest that viewers should feel something other than blind respect for the politicians who shaped their lives. The caricaturist's art—and choice of subject—invited official censorship: Daumier spent six months in prison for publishing his cartoon of King Louis-Philippe as *Gargantua*.[5] John Tenniel (1820–1914), whose illustrations of *Alice in Wonderland* and *Through the Looking Glass* remain bound in many readers' memories with the stories by Lewis Carroll, offered political and social commentary in the form of caricature through the pages of the periodical *Punch* (1841–1992).[6] A visual lexicon was being built and organized that, instead of requiring formal art education of its readers, called for experience with events of the day and, just as importantly, recognition of recurring visual elements across multiple caricatures. Juxtapositions of humans with symbolic beasts or in allegorical settings, with deformed or otherwise exaggerated body parts, and with melodramatic facial expressions were among the formal attributes through which caricature began evolving to cartoon.

In 1837, Swiss cartoonist Rudolphe Töpffer (1799–1846) created a book in which humorous pictures and minimal text combined to tell *The Adventures of Mr. Obadiah Oldbuck*. Characters and themes did not carry over from story to story, but each brief piece offered readers captioned cartoon images.[7] German Wilhelm Busch (1832–1908) published a picture book in 1871 that presented several different stories, depicted in image and verse, that featured the same characters. *Max und Moritz* details the misadventures of two naughty boys: they feed fowl connected strings, which causes the flock to hang itself; fall into a baker's dough machine and become baked into pastry; and so on. The images go beyond illustration that repeats verbal description by providing substantive information that is entirely missing from the text. Meanwhile, caricature had been imported as an intellectual concept to the United States, and serials dedicated to such satire made their appearance. In 1867, Charles Ross's *Ally Sloper* made the first of a long-running regular appearance in magazine and book format. In 1895, Richard Outcault (1863–1928) created the comic *The Yellow Kid*, over which the newspaper barons of the period vigorously competed.[8] Eventually, that cartoon developed from single-panel to multiple-panel presentation. Through *Ally Sloper* and *The Yellow Kid*, readers—and future creators—were introduced to a new storytelling method: the cartoon strip.

The invention of the comic book came about a quarter of a century later, a direct outgrowth of the popularity of newspaper comic strips. Although the comic book is considered an American invention, like jazz, practitioners abroad contributed to its evolution. Comic books were printed cheaply and serially by companies that both produced and distributed them. Their cheap production values induced comic book readers and eschewers alike to view the material as disposable and ephemeral. Across the 1920s and 1930s, several genres developed within what quickly became an industry. Publishers hired stables of creative and technical talent to produce comic books in syndicate-style arrangements that gave top billing to particular characters rather than to the artists or writers.

Wartime's political and social milieu encouraged creators and publishers to feature patriotic themes in addition to the superheroic fantasies, anthropomorphic animals, romance, and detective fictions already in vogue in American comic books—and, indeed, in American text-only dime novels. Cartoonists fused images and text to communicate for the war effort in a more direct way as well. The Army employed them to create sequential art that presented important information to military recruits, including how to load a rifle and how to practice good social hygiene.

Abroad, cartoonists in Europe and Asia were developing high-profile works. Hergé (1907–1983) first conceived of *Tintin* as a comic strip in 1929 and then rapidly moved the boy reporter to book-length serial adventures. At the end of World War II, Japanese cartoonists, led by Osamu Tezuka (1928–1989), developed their wartime exposure to Western comics into a form that reflected Japanese techniques and experiences.[9] Within the next thirty years, Japanese *manga* evolved into what is now internationally recognized as a specific approach to the larger medium of comics.

In postwar America, mature comics readers developed a taste for horror, an interest some popular culture scholars have connected to sensitivities of the atomic age. *Mad* magazine also appeared during that period, offering a vehicle for both cartoonists and satirists who developed a following that included diverse ages and levels of sophistication.

Along with the periodical *Mad*, newsstands distributed comic books featuring superheroes, cute animals, and romance tales. Publishing houses, distributors, and consumers focused on the product of the moment and gave no consideration to any interest today's issue might hold for readers in the future. Comics consumers purchased an inexpensive product that often was passed from hand to hand within a small group but was not perceived as potentially marketable to readers through libraries. Some comic books eventually became valuable collectors' items precisely because each issue was always the first and only edition, distributed for a limited time and withdrawn from public availability when the latest next issue was published.

Dr. Frederic Wertham (1895–1981), a German psychiatrist who took on the study of criminal behavior after he emigrated to the United States, published *Seduction of the Innocent* in the same decade that he supplied the Supreme Court with data that led to their monumental decision in *Brown v. Board of Education*.[10] Although his integrationist work was socially progressive, Wertham's *Seduction of the Innocent* was symptomatic of its conservative time, a simplistically stated screed against comic books as tawdry examples of lifestyle choices that the young would not have the wisdom to eschew. *Seduction of the Innocent* shaped the next era of comics publishing as well as public perception of comics as a commodity. Comic book publishers entered a period of self-censorship under the Comics Code Authority. The rubrics of that industry watchdog continue to hold sway today, applied to serial comic books that publishers intend for juvenile readership.

The conservatism of the fifties was followed by the inevitable swing of the social pendulum in the opposite direction as youth power erupted in the latter half of the sixties. Robert Crumb (1943–) turned from designing greeting cards to developing and exemplifying the underground comix movement. R. Crumb characters like Mr. Natural were intended to appeal, and did appeal, to hip adults, not to children. With themes that include drugs, sex, and rock and roll, underground comix are not just about being crude; they are about the life experiences and aesthetics of the immediately postwar and early baby boom generation. By presenting style and humor that echo a place, a time, and a popular cultural identity, comix gave young adults (and older ones who had an interest in modern artistic experiments) material that met them where they were, emerging from college campuses rather than from junior high schools.

Contract with God, by Will Eisner (1917–2005), published by Baronet Books in 1978, is generally regarded in both art and publishing circles as the first graphic novel. In fact, it is a book of short stories situated in one neighborhood and concerned with a particular set of characters and circumstances. It is literature told through sequential art bound to sequential narrative and intended to be complete within the book's covers.

Contract with God borrows from the distant and the near past and goes a step beyond what was, thirty years ago, the known world in publishing. The literary narrative derived its very cohesion—not just its mood or tone—from the fusion of image with word: the reader must comprehend both the load carried by each image and the content of the text in an ordered fashion and with continued reference between the visual and verbal components. *Contract with God* is not a single issue within a serial, and its noncommercial content is no more ephemeral than text-only fictions with similar themes, such as Henry Roth's *Call It Sleep* (Avon, 1964) or Mario Puzo's *Fortunate Pilgrim* (Random House, 1997). In fact, readers of any one of those titles might well appreciate the other two.

THE GROWTH
OF GRAPHIC NOVEL READERSHIP

Soon after Eisner reformulated the idea of comics to support the intricacies of a developed and complete literature, Art Spiegelman (1948–)

packaged sequential art in book form to create *Maus*, which presents the story of his father's survival during the Holocaust. He went on to win a special Pulitzer Prize for *Maus* in 1992.[11] The less-specialized reading public, in addition to comics-oriented readers, began to notice that the comics format could be used far more extensively than previous creators and audiences might have imagined. The inclusion of *Maus* in secondary-school and college curricula led to the coverage of Spiegelman's work in a variety of critical literary reference works that had not previously addressed sequential art.[12] Graphic novels were spreading from art departments and archives of popular culture to general library collections.

During the late eighties and through the nineties, publishers began to market graphic novels differently from comic books. Newsstands were disappearing from the American landscape. People who bought serialized comics had to look for new points of purchase. They most readily found what they were looking for at comics shops, game stores, and racks in some general merchandise outlets. Graphic novels and other highly produced volumes of retrospective comic strip material, however, are produced by book publishers and are distributed as such. Both the production and the distribution systems, which often involve small businesses, raise concerns that library purchasers need to address; those concerns will be treated later in this volume.

Readers of graphic novels have now had about a generation to develop their reading interests and to form acquisition habits. Libraries have used only about half that time to begin collecting for browsers and casual readers. (This excludes university special collections intended to provide exhaustive archives for academic examination.[13])

Members of today's audience for graphic novels have specific traits. They are sophisticated consumers of image-based communications, including film, television, and, more recently, computers. The boundaries of their world have expanded, and they are far more aware of popular culture outside their own national borders than their forebears ever were. They may be familiar with zines, the self-published works facilitated by ubiquitous and inexpensive photocopying opportunities. Certainly, zines have encouraged younger and female readers to explore graphic novels.

Graphic novel publishers, sellers, and reviewers struggle with the need to be aware of the wide variety of readers interested in their products, readers who—due to differences in age, ability, and personal taste—may have few topics of interest in common. Thus, the notion that the graphic novel is a *format*, rather than a genre, is important. People who read, or potentially would read, graphic novels may share little else intellectually or experientially, just like people who read magazines or watch movies. Graphic novels are hardly one-size-fits-all creations, as demonstrated by their presence in children's personal collections, teenagers' library selections, general and specialized bookstores, prison and hospital reading rooms, and book lists for English-language learners.

GRAPHIC NOVELS ARRIVE IN POPULAR LIBRARY COLLECTIONS

Over the past decade, public, school, and some special libraries have begun to formulate plans, policies, and procedures for meeting the needs of graphic novel readers. We are at a point now where we can examine those methods, highlighting what seems to be most efficient and effective, and identifying the issues that most strongly affect the maintenance of graphic novels in library settings.

Professional bibliographic attention to sequential art publishing, library treatment, and readership have each expanded over the past quarter-century. As far back as the seventies, a number of mainstream publishers were producing encyclopedias and directories featuring comics artists, information about specific strips, and the like. Libraries treated such volumes as reference material for people working in the visual arts or areas of popular culture. Some of those works have been revised and expanded since their initial publication.[14] They now are used by bibliographers, selectors, and students seeking information related to graphic novels they have read in courses in history and language arts, as well as in visual arts.

Less than fifteen years ago, professional interest in anything like graphic novels was limited to specialists concerned with cataloging comic books as serials and maintaining collections as collectibles.[15] Just a decade later, Stephen Weiner revised and updated his bibliography of recommended purchases for general library collections—and appended an essay on why graphic novels belong in libraries—to assist the growing number of librarians who had already made the decision to add the format but needed a shopping list for beginners.[16]

Since the publication of the second volume of *Maus* in 1991, reviews of graphic novels have multiplied in the standard sources libraries use.[17] Public, school, academic, and special librarians have formed electronic discussion groups to exchange ideas about graphic novels in libraries. In addition to industry and consumer sites, librarians and students in library schools create, maintain, and use the Web to provide their peers with bibliographic and programmatic assistance in selecting sequential art resources for general and specific user populations.[18] Professional organizations sponsor workshops and other presentations on the subject of incorporating the graphic novel format into libraries.

MYTHOLOGY AND THE GRAPHIC NOVEL

We live in a consumer-oriented, free-market culture. Those of us working in contemporary libraries have to keep abreast or even ahead of popular, technological, and bureaucratic evolutions in that culture, whether we serve the general public or a specific group, such as students in grades 6 through 8 or inmates of a state prison. Such realities should remind us to examine advice to determine how much of it is based on objective inquiry and how much of it is casual observation. The former saves us time and enables us to avoid the mistakes made by pioneers, whereas the latter can lead to a kind of professional mythology that hampers the development and implementation of the best practices that our libraries deserve.

When the subject is graphic novels, the rumors may or may not have some basis in fact. For now, however, the following stand as unproved myths:

> The graphic novel is a dying art form.
>
> Adolescents and adults who are poor readers can access graphic novels with ease.
>
> Students learning English for the first time will all enjoy and benefit from exposure to graphic novels.

Even if we were to ignore the implausibility of the first myth given that both our culture and the world are shifting to increasingly visual and mimetic forms of communication, we would have to admit that it is difficult to predict the death of any art form. Hindsight is the only credible way of identifying a particular art form's death. Are we serving our current users well if we deem media in which they have expressed interest to be dying? Does our prediction hasten its irrelevancy or simply frustrate those who expect us to provide for their cultural interests?

Because graphic novels contain both text and image that must be interpreted and understood in tandem, people with low literacy skills may not find them easy to access. The vocabulary of graphic novels is typically no less challenging than that of a traditional text targeting the same age group. The kind of abstraction that competent and comfortable text reading requires is also demanded by the graphic novel. In fact, to read a graphic novel successfully, a reader must consider input from two types of communication at once, abstract from each, and refer between them. Academic research on graphic novels and multiple literacies (visual, critical, etc.) is ongoing.[19]

Inspiring reluctant, unmotivated, or disaffected readers is another matter. Many projects have demonstrated the efficacy of graphic novels for some problem readers. That topic will be discussed more fully in the chapter on programming with graphic novels.

Additional factors must be considered before deciding to use graphic novels with English-language learners. Certainly many students new to English are not new to this art form. However, some students learning English come from cultures that proscribe depictions of some content or deem them distasteful. Before incorporating graphic novels into a plan of service for learners of English, evaluate the specific titles to be used and how their visual aspects may—or may not—resonate with the original cultures of the students to be served.

WHAT'S NEXT?

Chapter 2 provides a précis of the vocabulary shared by those who create, publish, collect, read, and market graphic novels. Using the vocabulary and constructs identified there, we will move to discussions of selection, bibliographic control, collection maintenance, pertinent programming, and such traditional library issues as intellectual freedom. Readers already familiar with the content of chapter 2 may want to use it as a reference when discussing graphic novels with colleagues and library users to whom the format is new.

Subsequent chapters address the practical concerns attached to combining a new format with an old institution. Given that both graphic novels and libraries are flexible and evolving entities, this book is intended to elicit dialogue and does not presume to be a retrospective analysis. Its goal is to increase and encourage continuing professional interest in making graphic novels available to readers through libraries. Working with graphic novels in libraries is still new territory. These chapters are maps that intentionally leave much room for future discoveries and innovations both within the graphic novel format and within libraries.

NOTES

1. Randall Scott, Sanford Berman, and Catherine Yronwode, *Comics Librarianship: A Handbook* (Jefferson, NC: McFarland, 1990).
2. D. Aviva Rothschild, *Graphic Novels: A Bibliographic Guide to Book-Length Comics* (Englewood, CO: Libraries Unlimited, 1995).
3. Scott McCloud, *Understanding Comics: The Invisible Art* (New York: HarperCollins, 1994).
4. National Archives (London), "William Hogarth," Learning Curve, http://www.spartacus.schoolnet.co.uk/PRhogarth.htm.
5. University of North Carolina at Chapel Hill and the Center for the Public Domain, "WebMuseum, Paris," Ibiblio: The Public's Library and Digital Archives, http://www.ibiblio.org/wm/paint/auth/daumier/.
6. National Archives (London), "Punch Magazine," Learning Curve, http://www.spartacus.schoolnet.co.uk/Jpunch.htm.
7. Don Markstein's Toonopedia (home page of Donald D. Markstein), http://www.toonopedia.com/oldbuck.htm.
8. Don Markstein's Toonopedia (home page of Donald D. Markstein) Accessed 28 April 2003. Available at http://www.toonopedia.com/yellow.htm.
9. Harry Kiyama, *The Four Immigrants Manga: A Japanese Experience in San Francisco, 1904–1924* (Berkeley, CA: Stone Bridge Press, 1999) offers readers the opportunity to consider both a clear predecessor of the modern graphic novel and the cross-cultural aspects of comics' evolving tenets from the onset of the twentieth century.
10. Frederic Wertham, *Seduction of the Innocent* (New York: Rinehart, 1956).
11. Although *Maus* appeared in serial form originally, its collection into two volumes, *Maus: A Survivor's Tale: My Father Bleeds History* (New York: Random House, 1986) and *Maus: A Survivor's Tale: And Here My Troubles Began* (New York: Pantheon, 1992)—and later into a single volume (New York: Pantheon, 1997)—shows it to be as complete a narrative as the novels of Charles Dickens, which also appeared serially before being reprinted as complete texts.
12. *Contemporary Literary Criticism*, vol. 76 (Chicago: Gale, 1993), treated *Maus*, as have many critical reference works since.
13. Bowling Green State University's Popular Culture Library was founded in 1969; Michigan State University and the Library of Congress are among other research libraries actively maintaining comprehensive comics collections.
14. Maurice Horn, *The World Encyclopedia of Comics*, rev. (Philadelphia: Chelsea House, 1999), and Frederik Schodt, *Dreamland Japan: Writings on Modern Manga* (Berkeley, CA: Stone Bridge Press, 1996), are among those that treat critical aspects of graphic novels as well as broader comics topics.
15. Scott, Berman, and Yronwode, *Comics Librarianship*.
16. Stephen Weiner, *The 101 Best Graphic Novels: A Guide to This Exciting New Medium* (New York: NBM, 2001).
17. See appendix A for possible sources of graphic novel reviews.
18. See appendix A for a list of useful websites for librarians working with graphic novel collections and concerns.
19. See, among other reports, Gretchen E. Schwarz, "Graphic Novels for Multiple Literacies," *Journal of Adolescent and Adult Literacy* (International Reading Association, November 2002), http://www.readingonline.org/newliteracies/lit_index.asp?HREF=/newliteracies/jaal/11-02_column.

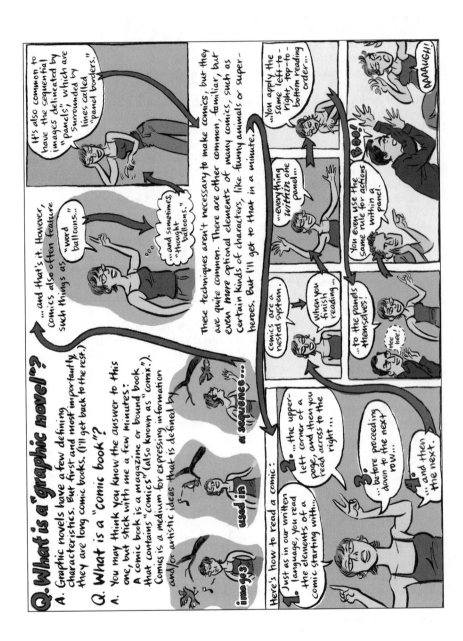

"What Is a 'Graphic Novel,'" by Jessica Abel, was first published on Artbomb. Visit the artist's website, http://www.artbabe.com, to download a PDF poster of this piece and obtain permission for its use.

CHAPTER 2

What Is the Right Word for a Book That Looks Like This?

Definitions

The graphic novel is part of a spectrum of sequential art formats that includes a range of related media such as one-panel gag cartoons and serially published comic books. However, to give graphic novels their critical due, I am focusing only on the graphic novel element of the spectrum, only on creative works that include narrative with a beginning, a middle, and an end and are published in book format.

To date, publishers and librarians have not devised a term to replace the misnomer *graphic novel* when referring to nonfiction. For now, then, *graphic novel* may be applied to works that are either factual or fictive. Further, a fictive graphic novel may be a single short story or a collection of short stories rather than a novel in the literary sense of a lengthy work that entails subplots and other complexities.

MAPPING THE TERRITORY

Graphic novels fit within several media spectra, just as ballads can be understood within the different realms of poetry, music, a period's popular culture, and storytelling. Each realm concerns itself with specific attributes that conform to aesthetic rules. To understand several realms enriches the audience's ability to appreciate a particular graphic novel—or ballad—but the audience must have a basic understanding of what at least one realm defines as necessary to the form in order to appreciate that particular instance of its realization. In the case of the graphic novel, we need to understand where it fits within the spectra of literature, art, and a particular culture (whether popular or ethnographic), and what literacy skills it demands of its audience.

Differentiating between Graphic Novels and Picture Books

Graphic novels are not a type of picture book; that is, they are not stories accompanied by illustrations that largely repeat the content of the written text. There is, of course, wide variation in the picture–book spectrum. For example, a picture book may be a story intended for young children, with text to be read aloud while the young listeners consider the accompanying images. Or a picture book can be a technical manual, for example, a book on knitting in which the drawings and photographs depict exactly how the bound-off handwork should look when the written directions are followed correctly. Or a picture book may be a compilation of high-resolution images that show the work of a particular artist or the visual details of a particular time or place.

The graphic novel indeed includes pictures, but the images must be integrated with the text so that *together* they provide a narrative that is richer than either element can provide alone. A child may leaf through her illustrated picture book and tell herself the same tale her father might read from its text—with more or less embellishment. A novice knitter will often refer to either text or image alone to ascertain how to move forward with a project. The photographs or plates in an art book are, of course, intended to be the viewer's primary focus, and the accompanying text is meant to supplement the images rather than to complete their communication.

The graphic novel is storytelling through, to use the term coined by Will Eisner, sequential art.[1] There is a beginning, a middle, and an end to the work as a whole, with each narrative moment a complex of word and image. Image and text refer back and forth to each other rather than repeat or supplement what has been communicated by the other. In this way, comics can be said to mimic mental processes. The graphic novel's presentation of images mimics the way we experience sensual data. The text works in the same way as our vocabulary in that it helps us to understand our subjective sensations. And just as our cognition derives from the interstices between sense data and sensibility's naming of experiences, so the graphic novel's story appears in the interstices between its images and its words.

Differentiating between Graphic Novels and Comic Books

Graphic novels employ several conventions developed through comic books. However, several traits differentiate the two forms. Comic books are serials, whereas graphic novels are often, but not always, contained within a single bound volume. Graphic novels presented in multiple volumes are nonetheless nonserial when completely published. A graphic novel presents a narrative that has a clear-cut beginning and end, whereas a comic book presents one episode in a limitless series and, as a result, the beginning and end of the series' universe are immaterial to the story at hand. Publishers produce—and libraries may subscribe to—comic books as they do other periodicals. Graphic novels, on the other hand, are published and selected as complete monographic works. That some graphic novels feature characters from comic books is important to note. However, categorizing is based not on characters but on the manner of publication—is an item a serial (that is, an episode within a boundless sequence) or is it independently complete and finite?

The Graphic Novel as a Format

The term *graphic novel* describes the format of a specific kind of publication. The format is a general plan of physical organization that can hold any type of content. Many different genres may appear as graphic novels, but the graphic novel itself is a format, or a medium, not a genre. The identification of a work as a graphic novel does not supply any useful information about content, but it succinctly describes form. One graphic novel may be a fantasy of interest and appropriate to teenagers, while another may be a romance suitable to middle-aged adults. In every case, the graphic novel medium incorporates the following formal aspects:

> The narrative is dynamic. There is constant reference between image and text, and both must be within the concern and literacy range of the reader.

The presentation is static. Action happens outside the images' depictions. This differs significantly from film, a medium that depends on the depiction of movement.

In the course of the narrative, change occurs, either through plot development, character development, or the passage of time in the work's universe.

FORMAL VOCABULARY

To be a literate graphic novel reader, one must be skilled at unpacking meaning from images and at decoding text. Literacy expands to include an array of visual conventions that are learned through practice and repetition just as textual conventions are absorbed by the competent reader of the printed word.

Creators and readers of comics have a developed format-specific vocabulary that we librarians need to use correctly if our bibliographic efforts are to advance access to graphic novels. Thus far we have taken a broad view of the graphic novel's formal territory. The definitions below supply some technical details.

The Anatomy of Comics

This first set of terms applies to the printed parts of the page. These terms are shared across the spectrum of comics, from the daily funnies to serial comic books and graphic novels.

Page   Layout shares the conventions of other print material. For Western publications, this means that information is presented in the same pattern that the reader's eyes move, from the upper left corner to the lower right corner of each page. Because nonprint media—particularly video—draw viewers' eyes toward the center of the field (the screen, in the case of video and computers), some printed pages may be designed so that the central idea is literally centered on the page.

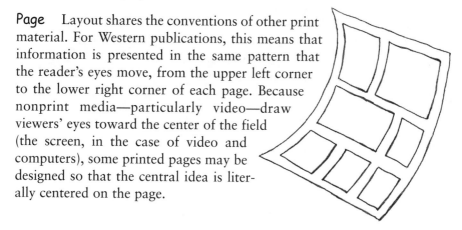

Panel   The bounded scene presents a
moment in the narrative. Panels are
often regularly shaped and contain
both image and text. However, panels need not be uniformly sized or
spaced. In fact, a panel's dimensions
and placement on the page impart
information about its content or
its relation to the moments
depicted in surrounding panels.

Gutter   The space between panels is a narrow, blank band that prompts the reader's
imagination to supply the action implied by the
static panels on either side. Sometimes gutters are
ruptured by an exploding panel or by overlaying
panels depicting rapid change or intensified drama.

Balloon   Spoken words are typically enclosed
by a rounded line, with a directional angle
indicating which character is speaking. An
author might be credited with composing the
characters' dialogue and the plot of the story,
but a graphic artist might be credited with
having lettered the words that
appear on the page.

Bubble   Characters' thoughts, if they must be disclosed to advance the narrative, are differentiated from words spoken aloud by the shape of their enclosure. The traditional shape in Western comics has been a kind of cloud trailing directional circlets toward the thinker, but other shapes that clearly differentiate thoughts—or iconographically depicted feelings or moods—may be used.

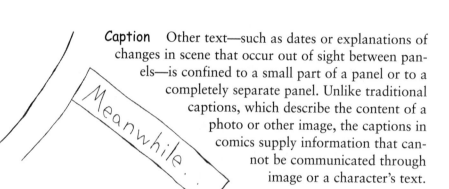

Caption   Other text—such as dates or explanations of changes in scene that occur out of sight between panels—is confined to a small part of a panel or to a completely separate panel. Unlike traditional captions, which describe the content of a photo or other image, the captions in comics supply information that cannot be communicated through image or a character's text.

Iconography   The meanings people attach to certain images and symbols are specific to their culture and reflect idiomatic speech. A character who is enraged, for instance, may be shown with a bolt of lightning sizzling near his head, while one stricken by love may have small hearts floating around him. Such symbols are purposefully stereotypical so that readers can absorb their content at a single glance, just as a traffic sign showing a skidding car quickly alerts drivers to hazardous road conditions, without requiring analytical reflection.

Onomatopoeia   Environmental sounds may be spelled out to accompany a visual portrayal. Thus a vase that has moved from the edge of the table in one panel to the floor in the next may have *crash* emitting from it at an angle. The lettering used to spell out such sounds may match the style of the image more closely than does the lettering used for captions and speech.

Visual hyperbole   Just as socialized people learn how to interpret others' facial expressions and body language, comics readers acquire an explicit understanding of various print conventions, such as the use of typographical symbols to denote swearing or of a lolling tongue and bulging eyes to indicate sexual attraction. Like iconography, the visual hyperbole found in comics differs in both content and emphasis from one culture to another. For instance, in a Western graphic novel the mouth is central in communicating emotion, whereas in an

Asian graphic novel the characters' eyes are significantly expressive. Background scenery also offers information about mood and narrative thrust, with some cartoonists revealing a character's thoughts or fantasies in some background images and his or her reality in others. Play with perspective, especially in *manga*, is another form of visual hyperbole.

A complete page, with all printed parts in place, is shown on page 23.

Sequential Art: The Extended Family of Comics

Sequential art, the name that Will Eisner gave to storytelling through images and words that continuously depend upon and refer between their content loads for complete meaning, includes media types other than the graphic novel. In the following set of definitions we consider how graphic novels fit into the larger realm of comics. The terms are arranged developmentally.

Dean Linnard

Cartoon   A single panel that provides the viewer with a visual pun, joke, or insight, the cartoon is put to use by editorialists as well as gag writers. Because the cartoon presents a single moment, no passage of time occurs within it and thus no narrative. A cartoon differs from an illustration by conveying unspeakable—or unwritable—information in image format. And any words in the cartoon could not be communicated through image. The cartoon depends upon the reader's understanding of social stereotypes as well as, often, information about another realm of discourse that generally lies outside the scene, such as current events or the behavioral norms of preschool-aged boys.

Cartooning   The act of drawing for any of the comics formats, from a newspaper's editorial page to a graphic novel, goes by the same term. In the production of most media within the comics realm, a variety of technical jobs exist, including penciler, inker, colorist, and letterer. The person responsible for writing the script, or plotline, or dialogue, need not be the same person doing the cartooning.

Comic strip   A regular feature of American newspapers, this form of sequential art usually appears in three or more panels. A comic strip has a given cast of characters that in most strips do not develop across time but go through a series of adventures with similar themes. The characters inhabiting Walt Kelly's *Pogo*, for instance, offered several generations humor and some sly political commentary, but neither hound nor possum aged, moved from swamp to city, or otherwise became what they were not already intrinsically at inception. Some comic strips, however, do support a developmental line in their story arc as they span years of serial publication. Even then, each day's strip, within the longer story arc, typically delivers a complete idea, joke, or ministory.[2]

Comic book   Comic books are serials, with regularly published issues in which single or multiple stories unfold. Several issues of a comic book that together present a full story may be republished in a single volume and treated like a graphic novel both bibliographically and from a merchandising standpoint. The inhabitants of any comic book universe may be organized into stories by different writers and cartoonists.

Comic strip album   Comic strips from newspapers and other serial sources may be republished in or out of sequence in bound albums. Unlike republished comic books in single-volume format, albums still contain many stories—or none, depending on the nature of the comic strips collected within—and the strips do not come to a conclusion beyond the winding down of a story arc that leaves the characters available to take up another, disconnected adventure.

Graphic novel   Unlike the cartoon, comic strip, or comic book, the graphic novel is complete within itself and provides a beginning, a middle, and an end to the story or information it places before the reader. However, it shares the earmarks of sequential art that comic books incorporate: image and word are bound together in order for the narrative to unfold.

BEYOND GENRES: POPULAR GRAPHIC NOVEL QUALIFIERS

Many genres of the graphic novel also appear in other literary and media formats: historical fiction, romance, science fiction, fantasy, realistic fiction, humor, and so forth. In addition, some genres are comics-specific, although their styles may be adapted for use in film and text-based literature.

Manga   The Japanese word for *comics* names a particular stylistic approach with its own iconography and visual hyperbole. The print format is related to the video format of *anime*. Not strictly a genre per se, this style can and does serve as a vessel for all manner of stories intended for specific and varied audiences.[3] However, conventions shared across bounds of genre differentiate *manga* from non-*manga*, including use of dramatic perspective, an elaborate visual vocabulary, and, more frequently these days, the maintenance of right-to-left orientation for titles translated from Japanese into English.

Superheroes   Borrowed directly from the classic comic book genre, this type of graphic novel features characters that are fallible in all ways save one. Whether they have superhuman strength, omniscience, or immortality, superheroes generally live as though they were merely human until precipitating events cause them to make use of their extra—and fate-changing—gift. Issues of political or moral power usually provide the underlying themes of such stories, regardless of their format. Some graphic novels use a comic book superhero (e.g., Batman) as a main character within a plot that is original and complete. Others may provide an original character whose superhero attributes are understandable to an audience that is familiar with the parameters of such fantasy.[4]

Role-playing   While the readers of comics and graphic novels enjoy a catholic assortment of interests and tastes, one subculture consists of fans of role-playing games (e.g., Dungeons and Dragons). Creators and publishers address the interests of this group through graphic novels that feature the characters, concerns, and worlds of specific role-playing games. Although such graphic novels might be read independently of participation in the related game, they are of greater interest to role-players than to the uninitiated. Role-playing games tend to have either a fantasy or a militaristic basis that the graphic novels naturally share.

Nonfiction   The most common subjects for nonfiction graphic novels are history, biography and autobiography, and popular science. In each case, both the critic and the reader must ascertain how factual the treatment actually is. Just as the line between fiction and memoir wavers, so too does the line between fact and fiction when information is expressed in a format that relies on both the writer's and the reader's creativity, on conventions that exploit stereotyped iconography, and on the interpretation of nonverbal content.

From here, we will apply our understanding of what graphic novels are to the development of graphic novel collections that address the needs and wants of library users and to recognition of the maintenance issues intrinsic to a graphic novel collection.

NOTES

1. Will Eisner, *Comics and Sequential Art* (Tamarac, FL: Poorhouse Press, 1990).
2. "Gasoline Alley," created in 1918 by Frank King, evolved in 1921 into a serial strip in which characters aged, entered new relationships, and even died. Other comic strips that present readers with characters who change and situations that develop in quasi-realistic ways are Lynn Johnston's *For Better or for Worse*, and Garry Trudeau's *Doonesbury*. Reading through albums of such strips clarifies how a particular story arc develops across days and weeks, and how characters age and develop across the years. Unlike a graphic novel, however, such albums reproduce story segments that are individually complete. Each strip can stand alone, outside the story of which, after its original publication, it has become a part, and the story's universe is unbounded by any end point.
3. *Manga*'s many genres include *shojo* (girls' comics) and *shonen* (boys' comics). Read by adults as well as youth in Japan, both are popular at present with teens and young adults of both genders in the United States.
4. A fine example of a superhero in graphic novel publishing is Paul Chadwick's Concrete. This environmentalist creature is featured in collections of short stories as well as in longer novellas.

CHAPTER 3

What Is Good?

*Finding Reviews
and Developing Collections*

*C*ollection development continues to be a professional activity that differentiates the library's mission from the missions of other agencies that deal with graphic novels. Unlike comics shops, the library works to balance collections in a variety of formats. Unlike bookstores, we attend both to replacing older works (where interest warrants) and to selecting new materials. Unlike archivists, we work to connect books with readers rather than strive to amass comprehensive collections that include all published examples of a format regardless of whether the examples speak to our users and would-be users. With graphic novels, as with other materials that we bring into our collections, we must be clear about their intended use, their evaluated worth to intended users, the prescriptions and limits of our budgets, and the relevance of weeding and replacement to the ongoing health of the collection as a whole.

The graphic novel format is relatively new (a quarter of a century) and its presence in libraries is usually much newer (a decade or so). Therefore, the collection development tools at our disposal are also recent creations. They continue to evolve in complexity and are sometimes in danger of being overlooked or underused.

BASIC COLLECTION DEVELOPMENT QUESTIONS: STILL RELEVANT

At the outset, a library planning to develop a graphic novel collection should identify and address all the basic questions that arise whenever any new collection is under consideration. Because the term *graphic novel* refers only to a format, it in no way defines the age, literary tastes, or aesthetic interests of the prospective target audience. In fact, American publishers produce more graphic novels for adult readers than for juvenile readers. If you plan to target teens with your graphic novel collection, you need to consider whether the library treats your community's teens as a separate, sophisticated group or as older children. If the primary users of your new collection will be postcollege young adults, you need to decide whether graphic novels will be purchased with money budgeted for adult fiction or for art books. If you intend to add graphic novels to an established collection that is broader in scope, such as the teen fiction collection, you need to determine whether the materials budget should be revised to identify graphic novels as a line item.

Those charged with developing the collection of graphic novels need to define the purpose and goals of their project to ensure that the process stays on track. Start with some basic fact finding by considering the following questions:

> For which members of my library's community will we be collecting graphic novels? Children? Adults? Teens? English-language learners? Adult literacy students? Users of the special visual arts collection? Several of those diverse groups or another group altogether?

> What does my budget allow? Do I have seed money to purchase a sizable start-up collection? Will ongoing funds be available for additions to the collection? Is a reliable source of money available to replace lost and damaged materials?

> Does my library's collection development policy already address issues related to graphic novels, or does it need to be reworked to accommodate that particular format?

Unless collection development staff begin by formulating conscientious responses to the preceding questions, they will find it difficult, and perhaps impossible, to bring together an intelligent and useful collection of graphic novels.

Collection Development Policies

Many collection development policies are intentionally broad enough to permit the acquisition of new formats, but others describe collection methods in format-specific ways and must be rewritten when a new format is considered. Appendix C provides sample collection development policies that include graphic novels within the library's plan.

LOCATING REVIEWS

As graphic novel collections become increasingly accepted in public, school, and academic libraries, more sources of reviews are addressing the needs of collection developers looking for authoritative evaluations of potential acquisitions. The following stalwarts of the collection developer's basic journal tools regularly include a handful of reviews of graphic novels:

> *Booklist*, published twice monthly during all but the summer months, includes graphic novels in its reviews for both adults and youth. An annual issue features graphic novels specifically.
>
> *Library Journal*, published twice monthly, publishes a regular graphic novel column by Steve Ratieri.
>
> *Publisher's Weekly* includes reviews of graphic novels for both adults and juveniles, and offers regular feature articles about trends in graphic novel publishing.
>
> *School Library Journal*, published monthly, includes reviews of juvenile graphic novels as well as graphic novels targeting adults but also appropriate for high school readers.
>
> *Voice of Youth Advocates (VOYA)*, published bimonthly, includes a regular column by Kat Kan on graphic novels of interest to readers in middle and high schools, as well as occasional reviews of new graphic novels for that age-group.

Given the relatively tiny number of graphic novels reviewed in each issue of the preceding journals, however, the collection developer will find the following additional source invaluable:

> *The Comics Journal*, published monthly, focuses on comics, including graphic novels, as an art form. In addition to

reviews, it provides industry information, interviews, and news about relevant events.

All of the preceding journals taken together, however, still will not provide enough timely coverage of the graphic novel publishing field to allow the collection developer to read about potential acquisitions while they are new and readily available for purchase. The collection developer must also turn to online reviews. For a continuous flow of newly reviewed options, the following sites are workhorses:

Artbomb (http://www.artbomb.net/books.jsp) offers staff-written reviews of new literary graphic novels available to American readers and archives its reviews for ongoing reference. Books are described in terms of story, art, and audience appeal. Cover scans (along with occasional hyperlinks to interior art) clarify written descriptions of appearance.

Diamond Comics Bookshelf (http://www.bookshelf.diamond comics.com/reviews/) features reviews written by Kat Kan, an experienced librarian and comics fan. Although this resource includes comic books as well as graphic novels, it supplies professionally acute, genre-diverse reviews and is updated regularly to include new releases. Appropriate age-groups are suggested for each title.

Grovel (http://www.grovel.org.uk) provides reviews of new American and British graphic novels. ISBN information is offered for both countries. Indexing access is by title, writer, and artist.

Ninth Art (http://www.ninthart.com) is updated weekly with new reviews, interviews, and other material intended for the critical or academic reader. The core contributors include comics writers and graduate students.

No Flying No Tights (http://www.noflyingnotights.com), with its sister sites, Sidekicks and The Lair, offers reviews and core lists of graphic novels. The original site is concerned with comics (mostly graphic novels) appropriate to teen readers. Sidekicks offers reviews of material suitable for younger readers, and The Lair focuses on materials that are best suited to adults and older teens. This site has been developed over several years by Robin Brenner, a library worker whose approach is consciously librarian-friendly as well as informative to teachers, parents, and readers of graphic novels.

Sequential Tart (http://www.sequentialtart.cm/reports.php) approaches the criticism of comics from a women's perspective. Monthly reviews can be sorted by such formats as graphic novel and by such genres as *manga*. The archives go back to 1998 and current reviews are updated monthly. The genre-diversified recommended reading lists in PDF format are an added bonus for collection developers.

Reading Graphic Novel Reviews Critically

When reviewing graphic novels for collection developers, a good critic will address appeal to the target audience, narrative cohesion, and visual and production quality. When relying on published reviews for the selection of materials, collection developers need to understand the limitations of the review process. No matter how brief the review (*Booklist* and *Library Journal*, for instance, allow the reviewer fewer than 250 words), the following matters demand critical notice:

Of what quality is the artwork and its reproduction?

How significant is the writer's choice of vocabulary, syntax, and other verbal details to the success of the work as a whole?

How well does the narrative flow?

Why is *this* story (or information) presented in *this* format?

CATCH PHRASES AS SHORTHAND

Understanding concise critical reviews in any specialized area depends on the ability to recognize the meaning attached to relevant catch phrases. In reviews of science fiction, for example, *space opera* carries a shorthand but relevant message. Reviews of audiobooks note whether particular recordings are *unvoiced*, *voiced*, or *semivoiced*. In reviews of graphic novels, shorthand references may address artistic styles, perceived level of sophistication needed to understand a work, and themes that may be controversial in some settings or communities.

In no case should such a catch phrase be so esoteric that an experienced review reader cannot immediately grasp its full meaning in the context of the reviewed material. In addition, if they are to be at all useful, reviews for libraries must be accessible to library staff. The purpose of catch phrases is to save print space within a review, not to obscure intended meaning.

Terms that describe artistic styles in graphic novels are listed below, with examples in parentheses:

- clear line (Hergé's *Tintin*)
- black ink or heavy black ink or saturated black ink (David B.'s *Epileptic*)
- blockprint-style (Kuper's *Metamorphosis*)
- scratch board (Ott's *Dead End*)
- saturated color (Pope's *Heavy Liquid*)
- watercolor (Talbot's *The Tale of One Bad Rat*)
- computer-enhanced or digital (Fuqua's *In the Shadow of Edgar Allan Poe*)

A reviewer's assumptions about the skills a reader needs to appreciate a specific graphic novel are subjective. Only by becoming familiar with how a particular reviewer perceives the differences between youth and adult levels of sophistication can a review reader come to trust—or reliably discount—such descriptions as "for mature high school readers," "only for the most sophisticated comics readers," and "for all fans of the format."

Unfortunately—but not surprisingly—one of the catch phrases often misused by both graphic novel reviewers and movie critics is *all ages*. Often, this assertion simply is not true. The item in question may be understandable by all ages, but it is unlikely to be of interest to all ages, at least not in the same ways or for the same reasons. *All ages* in our contemporary culture has come to mean "emotionally and politically safe," and that, indeed, is an evaluative judgment!

Even more cryptic are the coded terms reviewers use in the hope of warning away selectors whose readers (or whose readers' parents or grandparents) might find something offensive in the item under review. Most obscure are such warnings as *disrespectful of authority, irreverent,* and *strange*. More specific warnings are only as useful as you can make them by adding your own knowledge of your community's standards and your familiarity with works that broach similar themes. *Violence*, for instance, may be intrinsic to the subject matter, or it may be gratuitous. A reviewer needs to note the latter so that you can judge the appropriateness of a title for your prospective readership. In most cases, published reviews are not written by someone who knows your specific community, so any warnings must be taken with a grain of local salt, which only you can supply.

Like the graphic novel format and its inclusion in library collections, the review process for graphic novels is new and evolving. Over time, developers of graphic novel collections will grow to trust those reviewers who always acknowledge potentially sensitive issues. For now, with too few reviewers and relatively few venues for library-oriented reviews of graphic novels, many collection developers need to add to their selection tools. This may include turning to commercial vendors for assistance.

COMMERCIAL ASSISTANCE IN GRAPHIC NOVEL COLLECTION DEVELOPMENT

Three types of commercial sources can help the collection developer gather critical data about new graphic novels:

Publications from publishers and distributors of graphic novels. Such publications exist both in print and online.

Recommendations from library jobbers. These vendors have, in some cases, warmed to the concept of including graphic novels in their offerings and have developed lists that are intended to aid institutions in making selections.

Local retailers who stock and sell graphic novels. These professionals work with the same public that the library wants to target with its collection.

Although the collection developer needs to keep in mind that commercial sources of information may be motivated by profit, he or she should not automatically assume that they are pushing questionable material with a devil-may-care attitude. They may care more about their profit line than they do about the library public's best interest, but ultimately they are in the book business, so the collection developer has to assume that reading—and providing people with potentially good reading material—is important to them.

Publisher/Distributor Publications

The enterprises most intimately involved in the dissemination of graphic novels are those that mediate between the creator and the consumer.

Although graphic novels are produced by both small and larger publishing houses, the distribution system of many graphic novels—the means by which the materials move into the consumer stream—is relatively limited. Both publishers and the major comics distributor (Diamond) maintain websites that offer collection developers valuable information about specific titles.

In addition, some collection developers in libraries have turned to the same distributor-generated selection tool offered to comics stores. That paper publication, the Diamond Comics *Previews* catalog, is not a review source and should not be mistaken for one. Instead, it provides information about what is currently available for purchase. The intended target audience is the only evaluative information presented. And that target audience is based on the country as a whole, not on the standards in your community.

Nonetheless, the Diamond catalog furnishes a fuller picture of what is available and what is being sold to stores than do the standard review sources. Collection developers need such information to plan their local and limited collections realistically.

Library Jobbers

Many public and school libraries use the collection development lists created by library jobbers—whether those lists are standing orders or recommended purchase plans. Reputable library jobbers base their lists on critical input from review sources, professional input from the fields of publishing and library service, and marketing input from publishers interested in reaching the library market. They can alert the collection developer to a broader array of available graphic novels. And, unlike the comics distributor, library jobbers understand the issues involved in developing a library collection and realize that they must work to address libraries' concerns in order to maintain their business.

Local Retail Help

Not everyone has a full-fledged comics bookstore in town or nearby, but collection developers who do have good reason to make friends with the store's owner and employees.[1] An independent retailer must be savvy about the local market in order to maintain a profitable business and so should be able to help the library collection developer gain insight into the following key issues:

What are the demographics of the retailer's customer base? They may describe the library collection's target audience as well.

How much has the local market changed, and how much change is anticipated over time? Is the economy causing ups or downs in sales while the number of customers remains steady? Identifying the differences between sales figures and the numbers and types of browsers can assist the collection developer in discerning how economic indicators affect groups with an intellectual or aesthetic interest in graphic novels.

Which titles seem to be relative sleepers in the store but cry out for readers who do not frequent such a business? Those works belong in a library collection, where readers can find them over time and in connection with non-comics literature.

Who else in the community is well-informed about graphic novels and might be interested in advising a novice collection developer? Such individuals are most likely customers known to the retailer.

What are local preferences for specific genres or types of graphic novels? Are superheroes locally hot while *manga* languishes on a shelf? Or is the retailer having trouble stocking enough *manga* to keep customers satisfied? Such information can inspire the specific look of the local library's graphic novel collection.

Other ways in which the local comics retailer can contribute to the library's project to collect, maintain, circulate, and offer programming around graphic novels will be discussed later. However, the collection developer should keep in mind that such an establishment is an excellent place to compare published reviews with the reviewed material itself. If the collection developer is new to graphic novels and is unfamiliar with the catch phrases used in reviews, the retailer can demonstrate how the reviewer's words apply to a specific title.

There has been some debate about whether retailers who are helpful to libraries might be shooting themselves in the economic foot. In fact, one could strongly argue that libraries help such retailers. Communities with libraries where readers can discover graphic novels are developing devotees who often will, when financially able, turn to the retailer to acquire books to own or to give as gifts. By helping the library acquire a good collection, the retailer is addressing his or her own long-term interests in building a customer base.

GETTING READER ADVICE AND FEEDBACK

When considering the possibility of a new collection, libraries respond to various stimuli, including requests from the library's current users, staff interests, perceived community needs, and grant opportunities. The graphic novel collection's development shares some similar patterns with the development of media collections.

> It is more likely to be undertaken in a community where there is both public and staff interest in the format.
>
> Some members of the public may be better informed about the format than are many library staff members.
>
> The new collection may be planned as a means of attracting new or reluctant library users.
>
> The new collection must be expansive enough to withstand the initial run on its offerings.
>
> Users of the collection may respond to its presence in the library by suggesting additions.
>
> Library users unfamiliar with the format may have questions about its proper place within the library setting.

The collection developer should pay attention to each of the preceding points because they may yield key information for building and marketing a locally useful collection. Identifying current and potential library users who are knowledgeable about the format can help the collection developer to address true community needs and respect community standards. When consulting with collection advisors the library staff may need to take a firm stand on maintaining ultimate control over selections, however; that's an essential aspect of doing library work! Here are some methods for collecting and using input appropriately:

> Discuss plans to initiate or expand a graphic novel collection during outreach programs with the collection's target audience(s). For instance, during a book talk visit, ask students about their favorite comics or cartoonists.
>
> Recruit a focus group from the target population and ask them to create blurbs to promote some of the new additions to the graphic novel collection. If your library has an active book discussion

group or a Friends of the Library organization whose members might be interested in graphic novels, draw your focus group from those already-established organizations.

Make sure that the collection developer and the public service staff charged with maintaining the collection receive any patron suggestions related to the format. Respond to suggestions for purchase whenever they are relevant and affordable, and let patrons know that you appreciate their interest. Address community concerns about the collection or particular titles as they arise. Responding to community concerns will receive special attention later in this book.

GRAPHIC NOVEL AND OTHER RELEVANT AWARDS

As in other areas of creative expression, various awards may be given to published graphic novels. Collection developers need to track which titles are nominated for and win format-specific awards, who the award-winning artists are, and what other works have been created by those artists. Awards relevant to graphic novel publishing and lists of winning works can be found on the Comic Book Awards Almanac website.[2] Among these are the following:

Eisner Awards (1988–present) are made annually in nearly two dozen categories. Professionals in the comic book industry—including distributors and retail business owners—nominate and make the final selections in recognition of Best Writer/Artist, Best U.S. Edition of Foreign Material, Best Title for a Younger Audience, and so on. Graphic novels are eligible in several categories, but the ones specifically for them are Best Graphic Album—New and Best Graphic Album—Reprint.

Harvey Awards (1988–present) are made annually in twenty categories, none of which recognizes juvenile audiences. Comic book professionals nominate and vote on these awards. The categories specific to graphic novels are Best Graphic Album of Original Work and Best Graphic Album of Previously Published Work.

Lulu Awards (1997–present), determined by the membership of the Friends of Lulu, which is itself focused on promoting woman cartoonists, recognize cartoonists working in a variety of formats, including the graphic novel.

Reuben Awards (1946–present) are organized by the National Cartoonists Society into several categories addressing several media. The Comic Book Award regularly—but not always—goes to a graphic novel.

Collections should include material that has not yet achieved mainstream status. The role of the library is to educate as well as to provide recreation and information. Just as you would not collect histories published only by large, conglomerate publishing houses if you were trying to build a rounded and educating history collection, you should not omit efforts of smaller publishers in the realm of the relatively nascent graphic novel.

Xeric Foundation Comic Book Self-Publishing Grants (1992–present) assist comic book creators to publish their own works. Several publishers work with Xeric Foundation grant winners to distribute their work. Many artists who win Xeric Foundation grants produce graphic novels specifically. See http://www.xericfoundation.com/xericcomicgrants.html for annual lists of winning artists and the graphic novels published with the aid of Xeric grants.

Awards for graphic novels and other comics are made internationally as well, and sometimes English-language works win awards from such august organizations as France's Angoulême International Comics Festival, whose judges have, since 1974, bestowed honors in diverse categories, including works for children. The festival's annual Grand Prize honors a living person for his or her lifetime contribution to cartoons. The list of honorees (available at the Comic Book Awards Almanac website) includes a number of important graphic novelists whose work can broaden the cultural scope of your local collection. Groups whose main interest is in other forms of publishing may also recognize graphic novels and their creators. Two honors that are regularly presented to graphic novels are the Firecracker Alternative Book Award and the International Horror Critics' Guild Award for Best Graphic Novel. Special awards for specific graphic novels or their creators have on occasion been presented by the Pulitzer Prize Committee, the Hugo Awards, and Parents' Choice.

In addition to recognizing one graphic novel as the year's best, some organizations offer concise lists of graphic novels deserving special recognition by specific audiences. The Young Adult Library Services Association's Popular Paperbacks for Young Adults Committee has published lists of graphic novels for teens. In addition, that committee regularly includes graphic novels among the paperbacks on its various annual thematic lists.[3] As this book goes to press, a YALSA task force is formulating the structure of a standing selection committee dedicated to graphic novels.

Awards are indicators of popular or special interest, but collection developers need to be clear about how relevant particular awarding bodies are to their collection's target audience. In some cases, acquiring all of the nominated works in an award category may be just as important as maintaining copies of the actual winners. If the graphic novel collection is intended for a juvenile audience, then awards that do not consider juvenile readership may not be pertinent. However, creators may have other works that are appropriate to a younger audience, so check to make sure that your collection includes the works that are both relevant to your audience and recognized as comics publishing's best.

MAINTAINING THE COLLECTION AS A WHOLE

In addition to selecting the individual works in a graphic novel collection, it is important to consider the maintenance of the collection as a whole. Chapter 4 examines issues related to housing, identifying, and circulating graphic novels.

NOTES

1. Diamond maintains a web-based service for locating comics stores at http:// www.csls.diamondcomics.com. Although the service is less than perfect at recognizing and correlating zip codes, it can provide information about the proximity of local retailers and their types of products.
2. Among the resources available to the collection developer in search of retrospective citations of graphic novels is Joel Hahn's Comic Book Awards Almanac, http://users.rcn.com/aardy/comics/awards/index.html.
3. The YALSA lists, which include annotations, are available on the organization's website, http://www.ala.org/yalsa/.

CHAPTER 4

How Can I Deal with Pigeons from Hell?

Maintaining Graphic Novel Collections

The introduction and maintenance of a graphic novel collection requires both planning and ongoing communication with library staff about the format and its peculiarities. Issues about the graphic novel's physical attributes, such as shape and binding, that are relevant to library functions, such as shelving and circulation wear, must be resolved. Staff beliefs about the collection must be clarified and addressed. Whereas the previous chapter discussed the collection developer's tools, this chapter focuses on formulating processes that will enable graphic novels to have a healthy place in your library.

Certainly the first mistake I made with *Pigeons from Hell* at my library was that I neglected to make sure that any—let alone all!—of the issues had been addressed before I brought the work into the building.

THE NEED FOR A COMPETENT COLLECTION DEVELOPMENT POLICY

Collection development policies both inform and support staff and increase public understanding of what materials may be considered for—or rejected from—specific library collections and why. Every collection in a library—be it the children's music collection in a public library or the reference collection in a school library—is brought together for a purpose that the library must be able to state clearly and cogently.

Because youth services staff have been especially enthusiastic about including comics and graphic novels in popular library collections, there has been a tendency to treat the format as if it were age specific. In fact, as pointed out in previous chapters, the graphic novel is a suitable format for a variety of content of interest to people of various ages and concerns. Specific uses of the format are more appropriate for one group of potential readers than for another. Therefore, a library's collection development policy should identify the purpose and criteria for including graphic novels just as such policies address the inclusion of any other medium. Relegating a medium to a specific age-group undercuts the purpose of developing intelligent policy and shortchanges the medium.

Collection development policies for graphic novels need to address the following concerns:

> To which demographic group(s) are the materials targeted? Rather than spelling out ages or interests within a general collection development policy, this issue is best addressed by including graphic novels in pertinent subpolicies, such as those that describe the teen or children's or adult fiction collection. What should appear in the overarching policy is any criterion that is applied to every aspect of the collection and to all media. (For instance, the overarching collection policy might specify that your library supports the purchase of used materials or that it does not support the purchase of materials produced outside the United States.)

> Are selections based on specific aesthetic or pedagogical criteria? Although it may not be necessary—and can be confining—to spell out such criteria, doing so notifies policy readers that specific instances of the format are chosen over others, if that is indeed the case.

> Who selects the collection? Though a policy should not identify staff members by name, it may identify a particular position (e.g., librarian) or service area (e.g., art department). If the selectors of the graphic novel collection are the same as the selectors for the overarching library collection, no special

mention is needed. However, if some special or unusual choice underlies the designation of the graphic novel selector(s), it should be clarified in the policy.

Will the collection be composed of professionally selected materials only, or will any and all gifts be accepted? Given that graphic novels are currently underreviewed and fairly arcane, it may be unwise to promise to add whatever gifts are offered. And unless policies make it clear that materials are selected purposefully, it is hard to get a well-intentioned donor to understand that the mere fact that materials are "free" is not a sufficiently compelling reason to include them in the collection.

Must materials meet specific standards of physical condition to be added to or maintained in the collection?

Is balance among subjects or genres a consideration for the graphic novel collection as a whole? Is a particular genre (such as locally authored works) especially promoted?

Are materials liable to be deaccessioned if they fail to circulate at a prescribed level? If so, what is that level?

How will users be able to find materials added to the collection? Although collection development policies do not always spell out such information, both staff and users need to know that the collection is viewed as specific and definitive in some way. Knowing that the graphic novel collection will receive the same cataloging and display treatment as other collections reminds everyone that graphic novels are a legitimate and respected component of the collection as a whole.

The overarching collection policy should, of course, include clear statements about how suggestions and complaints will be handled. Complaints and suggestions for graphic novels should be treated like those for other media, and the procedures need not be spelled out separately.

Given that the graphic novel format is new to libraries and that its treatment by libraries is evolving quickly, collection development policies should be revisited frequently to ensure that they reflect institutional and publishing changes. Appendix C offers sample collection development policies from a variety of libraries where graphic novel collections are maintained.

INTERNAL MARKETING AND STAFF EDUCATION

Except for the tiniest institutions, most public, school, and even hospital and prison libraries employ people beyond the collection developer to maintain and circulate collections. Libraries serving medium and larger communities—whether civic, educational, or other agency-based—are likely to have formal staff positions for such tasks as acquisitions, materials processing, and circulation. In some circumstances, volunteers may staff some of those positions; for purposes of this discussion, such volunteers will be considered staff insofar as they make collections accessible to the intended population.

Given the newness of the graphic novel format, it is the rare library where all staff feel comfortable with and knowledgeable about the inclusion of such materials in the collection. Of course, there are some. I know of a middle school that includes a healthy collection of graphic novels in its leisure reading materials because the school's library media teacher—and sole paid staff member—appreciates them as pertinent to her users. Her support staff is composed entirely of middle school students whom she enlists to select materials, including graphic novels, for the leisure reading collection. Only an unusually independent-minded young activist who strongly opposed the format would suggest that it should be excluded, let alone initiate a campaign to dismantle the collection. But it could happen. With that possibility in mind, the library media teacher educates her proctors about why she includes specific material types, including graphic novels, in the collection.

In many libraries, few staff are informed and enthusiastic about graphic novels, many do not care, and some have strong feelings of distaste or even fear about their inclusion in the collection. Some of the negative opinions are cultural, and others spring from a personal predilection to stick with materials that do not require special physical handling. To minimize resistance, it is best to identify the potential issues and to educate staff before placing graphic novels in the acquisitions stream. If a new format is to become a successful part of your library's collection, who needs to know about it? Acquisitions staff, of course, need to know where the materials can be obtained reliably at optimal price and with minimal waiting time. Catalogers—if staff members—need to know where to find descriptive and classifying information. Making graphic novels shelf-ready is a large concern that is discussed later in a separate section. Shelvers and circulation staff will handle the materials regularly and will do a better job if they understand why the materials are in the collection. Those who perform readers' advisory functions with all library users, or with specific groups who are also target audiences for the graphic novel collection, need to be made aware of its presence, promise, and peculiarities as well.

INFORMATION NEEDS OF STAFF WHO MUST HANDLE THE COLLECTION

Staff who are responsible for purchasing, cataloging, processing, shelving, or circulating graphic novels have specific training needs if they are to do their jobs well. Make time to discuss the format with each staff group to address their concerns and determine what information they need to do a good job with the graphic novel collection. Acquisitions staff may need the name and contact information for a local comics retailer or an informed assessment of the capability of particular vendors to supply the graphic novels your collection requires. Catalogers who have not worked before with graphic novels may benefit from exploring online the cataloging work of staff at similarly sized and positioned libraries that have posted the descriptive and classifying treatment they have given to the graphic novels in their collections. Experienced shelvers know that different formats require different kinds of treatment to remain neatly on display. Discuss with your staff the types of shelving that will suit both the awkward dimensions of many graphic novels and the space available to contain the collection.

Educating Public Service Staff

Circulation staff, like other public desk staff, may find themselves on the receiving end of questions, comments, and complaints about library materials. Ask them to look at several graphic novels before the library's collection is unveiled—or, in the case of newly hired desk staff, soon after they start working in your library. Explain why graphic novels are important to the collection and valued by particular users. Encourage staff to direct questions to you rather than wonder silently or discuss their concerns with coworkers who are not responsible for the material's presence in the library.

Share graphic novel conventions with desk staff through entertaining book talks or shelf talks, either before opening or at general staff meetings. Invite staff at such gatherings to handle the graphic novels that are to be added to the collection. During casual conversations with other staff members, talk about graphic novels and include them in your reading recommendations. Explain what aspects of certain graphic novels you believe will appeal to a specific staff person, whether aesthetic, political, or genre. Demystify graphic novels for the rest of the staff rather than allow them to view the collection as your pet.

THE REALITY OF PRODUCTION PROBLEMS

Although some large commercial publishers include a few graphic novels in their lists, the library seeking a unique, truly diverse collection will have to turn to smaller, lesser-known sources for many of its purchases. This presents a series of challenges. A number of small publishers offer graphic novels that are of high literary or aesthetic quality, but production quality—especially when materials are to be circulated among multiple users—continues to be an issue. People building and maintaining a collection share a number of concerns about the physical limitations of many graphic novels, including

> extremes in volume dimensions, which include both folio and sub-mass-market paperback size;
>
> prevalence of paper covers over original hardback options;
>
> substandard gluing of pages to spine, resulting in premature loosening and loss of pages;
>
> preponderance of narrow spines that cannot support legible labels; and
>
> minimal gutters that preclude rebinding without loss of content.

Because many of the smaller publishing houses have no cash reserves for expensive upgrades, and because library concerns are relatively new to these publishers, library processing and mending departments must assume responsibility for solving substandard production problems. Some libraries cope with premature glue loosening by prebinding all their paperback graphic novel purchases, even when narrow gutters will lead to loss of content at the center of each page spread. A few well-endowed libraries make it a practice to purchase multiple copies of new graphic novels so that wear is shared across them during the title's circulation.

Another small-press-related downside is that the books go out of print rapidly. Replacing works that are only a few years old is a problem for libraries that maintain a variety of collections—hardcover mysteries and other genre fiction, for instance—but it is an issue for graphic novels as well. And because graphic novels are so often originally published in paper bindings, there is no second opportunity to purchase or replace an item when it moves from trade edition to mass market. Adding to the concern about ongoing availability is the fragile existence of the small publisher in today's economy: when a graphic novel publishing house goes out of business, its titles rarely go to another publisher for continued production.

This last issue is one that can serve the library collector well when he looks to a community-based retailer for support of a new library collection. The retailer must continue to turn over her stock, knowing that some titles would become staples if the graphic novel market had the stability of the more traditional publishing world. When the library adds such a book to its collection, the title can be viewed as saved from premature obsolescence.

To Bind or Not to Bind?

Some publishers, aware of new library interest in building and maintaining graphic novel collections that can be handled by diverse users and weather a multitude of rough circulation systems, are producing limited print runs of library editions that are hardback and often, but not always, bound slightly more sturdily than the traditional soft cover and glued binding editions. However, the overwhelming majority of graphic novels you will want to add to your collection will require some intervention by your processing or mending staff either to make them shelf ready or to salvage them from premature decay. People who have worked with libraries' graphic novel collections over the past decade have used a number of strengthening techniques.

Lamination   Some processing departments simply laminate the exterior covers of newly acquired paperback graphic novels. Although this aids in keeping the front and back of the book relatively tidy, weak spine glue must then support the added weight of the plastic lamination.

Prebinding   Both vendors and individual libraries sometimes opt to prebind materials that are available only in paperback format. Some companies do an excellent job of maintaining the original cover as a layer within the hardcover prebind. Often, however, books with such prebinding do not lie flat when open.

Strengthening the spine Stapling, regluing, and taping are all used by libraries to resolve—or try to resolve—the prevalence of weak spine glue. Unless done by a real expert, these techniques almost always lead to loss of the gutter and even part of the text near the gutter. Stapling, like prebinding, also usually confounds the reader's attempts to lay the book flat when open. Many libraries save the work of the mender until damage has occurred. Graphic novels that have loosened pages or paper covers decayed at the corners are referred to the mender, who then works to rebuild the damaged area. In some cases, this use of human resources may be preferable to prophylactic attempts to build up the product at the beginning.

Tipping in loose pages Taping or regluing individual loose pages puts less stress on the spine than does stapling or regluing the book as a whole when new. However, depending upon the price of the individual graphic novel and the amount of work required to mend it, replacement may be a cheaper and more timely option.

Repairing bindings Once a heavily circulating graphic novel begins to shed pages, it may need to be sent to a professional bindery. Especially in cases where a work is no longer in print or available, paying the cost of binding may be preferable to losing the book or some of its pages. However, given that professional binding is expensive, it should not be done on material that should be deaccessioned because it is worn out and of no continued value to your library's users.

Building up covers Professional and judicious use of cardboard and laminating material, or of heavy-mil plastic covers, may be a suitable alternative to complete rebinding.

Additional Processing Issues

To make library materials easy for users to find, some type of additional labeling is placed on their exterior surfaces. In the typical modern American library, a graphic novel is likely to sport, at a minimum, a spine label, a bar code sticker on its front or back cover, and perhaps an exterior date due slip. Because graphic novel covers present important visual information to the browser, the placement of so many bibliographic control pieces will often be problematical. Similar difficulties occur in the library's picture book collection, where browsing prereaders must cope with cover illustrations or endpapers that are marred by stickers that confound the artist's message.

A radical solution to this problem is to except graphic novels from the usual stickering treatment applied to the rest of the library's collection. However, we live in a mechanized and routinized world in which circulation procedures would be badly compromised if exceptions were made whenever library materials were deemed sacrosanct from blemish. Nonetheless, where a graphic novel collection is small and library staff are sympathetic, it may be possible to arrange for the materials to be treated specially.

The rest of us simply must accept that, for now, typical library practices include standards for marring specific areas of a book in order to make it available to prospective readers. As new technologies evolve, ways may be found that allow the graphic novel collection to remain visually intact. The controversial radio frequency identification security and circulation system (RFID), for instance, may spell the end of the need to place barcodes on book covers.

SHELVING CONCERNS

Many graphic novels fall outside the standard dimensions for mainstream book publishing. Some graphic novels are folio sized but quite slim, while others are thick but diminutive in surface area. Due to the preponderance of paper binding, graphic novels require substantial buttressing if they are shelved in the traditional spine-out fashion. And because most graphic novel collections tend to be heavily browsed, the shelves that hold them are in almost constant need of maintenance in order to appear tidy. When library materials are left to fall, then be pushed and restacked by browsers, damage is more likely to occur.

A variety of approaches to shelving issues are in use today. Identifying the ones that may work best in your library depends in part on the magnitude and intent of your graphic novel collection. If you have graphic novels but are not shelving them separately from other fiction or nonfiction, then intershelving them with sturdier volumes is likely to keep them buttressed and safe. However, they will be difficult to browse as a medium, and library users will not perceive them as a collection.

If the graphic novel collection—or some generous portion of it—is to be shelved together as a media format, the following issues need to be resolved:

> Where will the collection fit? Are the designated shelves spaced widely enough to allow extra-tall graphic novels to stand up, or will they be inverted to rest spine up?

Is there space and facility for shelving the collection face out? If so, can enough order be maintained to enable users to find specific titles?

If the collection is to be shelved spine out, are there enough bookends on hand to allow insertion at short, regular intervals? Or does the library have available special shelving that has built-in metal slats at regular intervals?

Who will maintain the physical collection? How frequently will they shelve returns? How often will they reshelve browsed materials in the appropriate places?

In later chapters, we will discuss the placement of the collection in relation to neighboring collections as well as the marketing merits of face-out and spine-out displays. Here the concern is handling the material efficiently and effectively. Among the techniques some libraries use to improve the shelving of their graphic novel collections are the following:

Park a book truck near the collection and ask that browsers place graphic novels on it instead of trying to reshelve the materials themselves.

Use display shelving, rather than standard shelving, for housing the collection. Rotate additional titles into the display on a frequent basis, perhaps as often as daily.

Arrange the collection, if small, in plastic crates through which browsers can flip, and place the crates on tables.

Apply rough-sided utility tape along the length of metal shelves to forestall the collapse of volumes when several are off the shelf at once and no bookend has been adjusted to prop the line.

Repair worn spine tape and label lock stickers so that roughened edges do not catch on each other when individual volumes are withdrawn from the shelf.

Use a volunteer who enjoys graphic novels to perform shelf maintenance more frequently than regular staff does for other, more easily maintained collections.

If staffing permits, provide training for those who are most likely to shelve graphic novels on a regular basis. Apprise them of the issues both for their own education and to acknowledge that you are aware that shelving graphic novels involves additional details.

THEFT AND VANDALISM

Whether graphic novel collections are prone to abuse by adoring—or disapproving—library users is a long, ongoing discussion. The very fact that libraries "spoil" the mint condition of new comic books with property stamps, barcodes, and so on detracts from their monetary worth in a good way. Once a library has stamped, stickered, and perhaps even stapled a graphic novel, its street value is reduced below the level of bother for individuals who are wont to plunder attractive wares for resale at flea markets.

However, some reluctant users may be tempted into the library after a prolonged absence by the very presence of the new graphic novel collection. Especially in the case of young adolescents, these folks may have library card records so far in arrears that they are reticent about using the prescribed circulation methods. And, of course, materials "borrowed" without being recorded are less likely to be returned. The pressures of a due date or dunning notices may be avoided, but the level of shame about stealing is likely to prevent that "borrower" from returning the goods to the source.

The ubiquity of cheap photocopying and the availability of the Internet, with its abundant and easy access to cartoonists' artwork, seem to have spelled a decrease in the number of vandals who cut or tear a particularly attractive page from library materials just to have it as their own. Nonetheless, graphic novels are not safe from vandalism. The most common interference may be the "misshelving" of material by someone—either staff or library patron—who deems a work offensive but is unwilling to mount a direct challenge. Depending on your library's typical clientele—elementary-school children, professional-club members, hospital patients—you are probably already alert to specific levels and patterns of vandalism. Now consider how the features of graphic novels may or may not relate to those patterns. For example, young children may feel the urge to apply crayon to black-and-white images. Address vandalism when it occurs, but there is no reason to expect that the graphic novel collection will be especially vulnerable to such behavior.

BEYOND MAINTENANCE TO ACCESS

Concerns about potential users' access affect all your collections, and the graphic novel collection sports its own set of special needs. Will your library's users be able to find graphic novels in your catalog? Where in your library's building will users need to travel to find graphic novels? The next chapter explores various access issues that need to be addressed to ensure that your graphic novel collection plays an active role in your library.

CHAPTER 5

Can Readers Find Your Library's Graphic Novels?

Classification and Descriptive Cataloging

No ethical professional wants to see a collection being built and maintained without being known to its intended users. Browsing collections are composed of materials of similar format brought together with the expectation that users value being able to sort through the items right then and there rather than working to identify what the library owns and then ascertaining whether it is currently available. Simply browsing may be an enjoyable activity, but uncataloged browsing collections can frustrate library users because they do not indicate if or how one item in that collection may be related to another item—sharing an author, a subject, or intellectual content. Though it may be tempting to bypass cataloging materials that are so popular that they do not stay on the shelf for long, only inveterate browsers are served by such tactics.

Among the prospective users of your graphic novel collection are bound to be people who have not previously used the library or who do not look at the library's catalog—either inside the building or remotely—to determine whether it includes material of specific interest to them. There are also people who are already interested in the format and want to know which specific works the library owns rather than simply what materials are on the shelf today.

When opening or expanding a collection of any sort, there is no advantage to the public—and rarely any advantage to the library—in keeping the collection out of the catalog. Now that most public and school libraries have computerized catalogs that can provide accurate circulation statistics—and that can usually be viewed remotely by prospective library users—such institutions can ill afford to invest in a collection without also investing in making that collection evident to its potential users.

CATALOGING GRAPHIC NOVELS

Graphic novels have become so prevalent in libraries that catalogers, as well as collection developers and readers' advisors, are actively working to give the format the professional attention it requires. Nonetheless, current practices remain widely varied.

As this book was being written, the Library of Congress invited librarians in the field to participate in a formal discussion of the appropriate placement of graphic novels within the Dewey Decimal Classification system.[1] Many of the largest public libraries—and perhaps library jobbers who provide cataloging with materials purchased—may or may not follow the Library of Congress's current Dewey prescription. Other libraries use the Library of Congress system when classifying all of their materials, including graphic novels. And there remain libraries that use alternative systems to impose order on their collections—including the eccentric coding of acquisitions so that each item's shelf order simply reflects when it entered into the collection.

One of the liveliest topics on electronic discussion lists serving librarians interested in graphic novels is how both the collection and its potential users may best be served by various classification strategies. Although the approach any one library takes should at least relate to the technical decisions made for its other collections, a variety of classification systems specific to graphic novels are employed with more or less arguable logic. For example:

> Format goes unconsidered and individual titles are treated according to intellectual content alone. In this plan, a graphic novel that is nonfiction would be located by Dewey or Library of Congress classification number among traditional print titles addressing the same subject. Graphic novels that are regarded as fiction would likewise be placed in the fiction, or science fiction, or short story collection—either in the literature classification or, as numerous libraries maintain their fiction collections, according to the author's surname.

Format dominates and trumps all other aspects of any individual title. As a result, libraries that use Dewey as the standard classification scheme place all graphic novels in the call number area of 741.5, as though they were caricatures, comic books, or comic strips. Although the Dewey schedule allows for considerable subdivision,[2] most libraries do not take decimals beyond a single digit to describe graphic novels.

Graphic novels are awarded a category of their own—perhaps with a straightforward title like "Graphic Novel"—and are organized without reference to other collections' possibly shared characteristics (such as subject or author).

Graphic novels go untreated by cataloging staff and can be used only as a browsing collection.

Cataloging for Systematically Open Access

Collections should be housed so that materials that share common qualities are grouped together. Materials that have not been classified or organized in any bibliographic manner are less likely to be found by users and are less likely to fulfill any user's needs.

Joining classification methods with housing options creates a powerful dynamic. Not only can users easily access materials, but they can also see how those materials relate to others. Of course sophisticated library users and readers may look for such relationships automatically, but providing access to such connections expands any user's frame of reference and intellectual experience.

Graphic novels may sometimes be dispersed throughout a collection of materials in similar formats (such as traditional print books). In this situation, the graphic novels should be given the same classification and descriptive treatment as the materials among which they are to be dispersed. For instance, if all such materials are organized by authors' names, then the graphic novels should be fit into the group according to authors' names (not according to publisher or ongoing series name). If all such material, however, is arranged by Library of Congress call numbers and it has been decided that the few graphic novels in the children's collection are to be treated as fiction, then those works would be further sorted to reflect whether their authors were French or Japanese or American.

Clearly, such a scheme will not allow a user to find others "like this"—where the "like this" refers to format—simply by browsing. For that reason alone, it seems unsupportable to force graphic novels into such a format-blind classification system. However, if the cataloging includes a format descriptor among the item's subject headings (if, for example, it includes the term *graphic novels* in the MARC tag field 655), a library user could at least find others "like this" through the catalog.[3] And if there is only a handful of such items in a collection of hundreds or thousands of others, it may be more practical to turn a blind eye to format as an issue of any note beyond a mention in the subject heading.

CURRENT CONTROVERSIES IN CATALOGING GRAPHIC NOVELS

The use of Dewey number 741.5 as the proper place for graphic novels currently provokes a lively argument among catalogers and even some users of graphic novel collections. On the one hand, such classification reflects aspects of the material's format and brings all materials of a similar format together within a larger collection. Nevertheless, 741.5 seems too broad a classification, and it recognizes only some attributes such materials share. Among the problems with this classification assertion are

inadequate differentiation of independently conceived and plotted works (that is, true graphic novels) from works that belong to an ongoing series produced by a publisher's changing stable of artists (comic book series) or collections of discrete moments of a comic strip brought together within an album;

lack of distinction between fiction and graphic novel–style nonfiction; and

sloppy conceptualization of the differences between comic strips, comic book serials, graphic novels, and information about working in one aspect of graphic arts.

The move toward providing graphic novels with a call-number prefix of their own warrants continued observation and analysis. Like the prefix *picture book* used in some libraries, the prefix *graphic novel* may end up swallowing too many distinctions, especially if it encompasses fiction and nonfiction, compilations of previously published serials, and illustrated books for older readers. However, the format-specific prefix *GN*, like the format-specific prefix *DVD*, may be useful in communicating format only, when the size of a graphic novel collection warrants it and when full cataloging provides further analytical detail, through specific call numbers and subject headings, to place materials within a multifaceted graphic novel collection.

Such a scheme brings order to the graphic novel collection as a whole much as it brings order to many other collections within a library. In addition to logically connecting the parts (specific titles) to the whole (collection), such a plan reflects the diversity of topics that can be undertaken in graphic novel discourse.

DESCRIPTIVE CATALOGING

Whether the library employs its own professional cataloging staff or outsources those tasks, users of all its collections profit from content descriptions that indicate how any one item in the collection may be related to others. Full cataloging offers precisely such intellectual contextualizing. Full descriptive treatment makes it easier for web-based catalog users to find materials because it enables them to employ a variety of search strategies.

Graphic novels are hardly unique in their need for multiple descriptive access points. A parallel case can be made for treating the library's juvenile picture book collection or DVD collection as worthy of classification and consistent descriptor sets so that users have more information about content than they might glean from the title; know who is responsible for the intellectual, artistic, and commercial reality of any specific holding; and have the ability to find similar items based on any of the descriptors.

Depending on the current size and planned growth of the library's graphic novel collection, analyzing and describing its contents may not be worth a cataloger's time and expertise. However, if the collection is expected to grow beyond an experiment for browsers, full descriptive cataloging, including analytics and careful differentiation of the various comics-related media—comic book series, comic strip compilations, and true graphic novels—becomes pertinent to maintaining the collection's usefulness and accessibility.

Subject Headings and Cataloging Notes

Many libraries with collections that include graphic novels—as well as library jobbers who provide cataloging with purchased library materials—

use either *Sears List of Subject Headings* or *Library of Congress Subject Headings* as the authority by which the contents of titles are described.[4] Graphic novels need the same attention as other materials when applicable descriptors are chosen from the subject headings. Due to the recent interest of several libraries with on-site catalogers and of library jobbers that sell graphic novels with cataloging included, many graphic novel bibliographic records are available through the Online Computer Library Center (OCLC) for other libraries to use as the basis for copy cataloging.

Describing the format as *graphic novel* in both the call number and the MARC record's subject fields is a redundancy that is necessary to draw the attention of catalog users who are searching by any field. (Similar redundancy occurs when libraries include the recording format as a specific MARC tag and use the format name as a call number element, as with DVD collections or compact disc audiobook collections.) Beyond that, tracings should reflect aspects of the graphic novel's specific content, subordinate creators, and subject headings appropriate to your community (such as *manga* where that genre is popular). Notes should be included to supply further useful details about the graphic novel. For example, a note specifying that a graphic novel is unflipped informs potential users that the material is to be read right to left.

Literary genre subject headings improve the chances that potential readers will enjoy the format in general, especially if they are more enthusiastic about certain narrative types (for instance, mysteries) than others (such as science fiction). And during busy public service times, when readers' advisors may have to rely on the catalog, they will find it helpful if subject headings provide as much information as possible about form, style, content, and connections to other works.

Bibliographic Information or Advertising?

Several publishers of graphic novels apply an age-rating system to their titles. The underlying theory is that such a system might help consumers ascertain the appropriate target audience for a work, but the age ratings are general, national, and speculative. Publishers of mainstream juvenile books typically identify an assumed audience age range, often on the inside flap of the paper dust jacket or in some other discreet area of the book. While the age ranges for juvenile books would not be copied into most catalogs as pertinent bibliographic information, the age ratings for graphic novels sometimes are.

The inclusion of publishers' age ratings should be deeply considered before it becomes a standard practice. Are other collections in your library cataloged to include such information in each record? Are the movie industry's ratings placed in the records of the videos in your library's collection? Are both staff and users clear about the library's intent in prescribing audience ages? Does such information serve a positive purpose, or is it included in order to provide complete details about title page information?

Does the graphic novel publisher share your community's view of what level of sophistication can be expected from most readers at specific ages? Is the material placed in a collection defined as serving the specified age-group? How do you expect staff and library users to understand any mismatch between the publisher's age rating in the record and the item's placement in the larger collection?

Will information about age have a chilling effect on the circulation of the material? Will it influence circulation or interest in other ways?

Certainly the inclusion of such data in the cataloging record opens the way for someone to assert that a reader or borrower deemed underage by the catalog has gained access to the material nonetheless. It also creates an opportunity for library users to object that the library is prescribing and proscribing specific titles for specific readers.

Educating the Cataloger

When working with graphic novels, some catalogers may need instruction in how to recognize germane details for local tracing in the catalog. For instance, if *manga* is a local subject tracing, does the cataloger recognize the features of that style? When sequels and prequels are not listed on the item itself but are of interest to the prospective catalog user, the cataloger may need to obtain the information from a preexisting OCLC record or another source.

Many technical services staff prepare materials for public access without regularly experiencing public service firsthand. In a library that depends on the cataloger to make graphic novels accessible through the record display, a member of the public service staff may need to assist the cataloger in learning how to fully describe and appropriately place graphic novels within the larger collection. The cataloger needs to understand that the graphic novel, like any other book, requires full bibliographic treatment. The following aspects of that treatment, however, are specific to graphic novels:

- the need for including multiple artists and designers to fully describe creative responsibility for some works
- the need for consistency of placement within the collection, whether to a special call number, to a part of the Library of Congress or Dewey schedule, or without regard to format
- understanding that materials do not always open at the traditional access point
- acquiescence to the selector's decisions about age-level placements

The last point is a concern that many library staff may feel the need to discuss with the selector. Those who stand outside the effort to develop the graphic novel collection and who do not read graphic novels may assume, due to the books' image-heavy nature, that the intended audience must be teenaged or juvenile. That assumption has led and continues to lead some libraries to place all their graphic novels at one age-specific location (such as the young adult collection). Two collecting problems can result: (1) the collection contains material that is inappropriate for its intended users, and (2) the library fails to collect from the vast array of graphic novels that are not appropriate to the designated age group.

Either situation skews the graphic novel collection. That is why it is important for cataloging staff to understand that the format itself is appropriate for all ages but that the content of one book may be geared toward one audience or age-group while the content of another may be geared toward a different audience.

TRANSLATION ISSUES CAN INFLUENCE ACCESS

A healthy graphic novel collection is likely to contain material from many comics-producing cultures. A variety of publishers are bringing contemporary European graphic novels to American readers. The Japanese *manga* tradition has spread to other parts of Asia, and so here we can peruse comics with Korean and Chinese roots as well as Japanese. Building a robust collection representing many cultures gives rise to translation and interpretation issues for both catalogers and readers.

Tintin's Characters as a Translation Case in Point

Hergé's series of fiction in sequential art format about boy reporter Tintin offers a good case study of how translation and interpretation can work both to change and to stabilize the content of a graphic novel as it moves from language to language. Many of the characters peopling the pages of *Tintin* books—including his dog Snowy, the twins Tompson and Thompson, and Captain Haddock—bear names that seem to be visual and cultural puns in English. But Hergé wrote the books in Belgian French, so our versions are, indeed, linguistic and cultural translations. And the books have been dynamically translated into many other languages as well—Tibetan, Russian, Greek, and Portuguese, to name a very few—with the puns intact. Of course, to maintain the puns and cues from language to language, the names had to be *interpreted* rather than literally *translated*.

Visual Cues Are Culture-Specific Too

Visual aspects of well-translated graphic novels are also interpreted. The trend toward publishing English-language versions of Japanese *manga* so that the story moves from right to left, as it does in the original, ensures that American readers will not be faced with a surfeit of left-handed samurai.

Although name changes in a translation will not bother a cataloger or processing clerk, a translation that opens from the left and sports its title on what is typically the back cover can present problems. When libraries apply bar codes or other item-specific labels to a particular area of a book (e.g., the top left corner of the front cover or the inside center of the back cover), tagging may appear in unusual spots on translations, perhaps obscuring information that would be perfectly visible if the book were in a typical English-language format.

Making Realistic Local Decisions

How to shelve books published with a right-to-left orientation—and thus with a front cover where most expect to see the back—must be addressed when collecting begins. The alternative is to stump several shelvers, each of whom may devise a personally distinctive method, most of which (spine *in*?) could lose the book to any potential reader.

Technical and public service staff who work with the graphic novel collection should discuss their concerns about materials that have non-standard orientations. On the one hand, there is the very real need to maximize workflow. On the other, there is the equal demand that all materials be treated in ways that keep them from being perceived—either by library staff or library users—as inferior. Full discussions between the graphic novel selector and the technical support staff that standardize collection access must address the physical anomalies as well as the intellectual concerns presented by the graphic novel collection. Appropriate treatment of such materials will require local decision making based on staff skills, the technology in use, and the ramifications that technology has for the material and its users. These are real and urgent issues that call for thorough discussions and thoughtful decisions.

The Next Collection Frontier for Your Library?

Because different cultures have differing attitudes toward graphic novels and comic books, the publication of such materials varies from nation to nation. Your library may already maintain collections of materials in Japanese and Chinese that include volumes of sequential art. Graphic novel publishing is also healthy in France, and, depending on your local demographics, you may have acquired the original texts of some recently popular French graphic novels.[5] If your graphic novel collection includes works that appeal to teens and young adults, you may already be aware that some of them are so interested in accessing comics in their original languages that they actively seek the untranslated versions.

Strive to guide users of your library toward all the collections that include material types in which they are already interested. For youth, if you have a strong Japanese collection maintained for native speakers, you may want to publish paper or online book lists that include references to that alternative source of *manga*. If you have an international language collection through which graphic novels are scattered, you may want to find a suitable subject term that will enable catalog users to identify graphic novels within those collections.

DOCUMENTING BEST PRACTICES

The discipline of treating the bibliographic elements of the graphic novel collection continues to lag behind the building and marketing of such collections. As both libraries and library users gain experience with the graphic novel, concerns about technical services will evolve more fully. To contribute to that process, those working to make graphic novels accessible within a collection are encouraged to communicate about their efforts through such professional channels as local and national library associations and policy bodies.

In the next chapter, where we now turn to the topics of marketing and promotion, the importance of graphic novel cataloging becomes evident. Both the clarification of format issues and the redundant content access facilitated by excellent cataloging can ease the efforts needed to make the graphic novel collection visible and attractive to potential users.

NOTES

1. In 2004, the Library of Congress announced a discussion on the treatment of graphic novels. See http://www.oclc.org/dewey/discussion/papers/ graphicnovels.htm for its opening proposition that this specific format be combined with comic books, comic strip collections, and other cartoon-based print works.
2. The draft schedule offers a refinement of graphic novel placement that accounts for genre, nationality, and style (such as *manga*) if the cataloger provides as many as five places beyond the decimal point. See http://www.oclc.org/dewey/ discussion/papers/GraphicTestNov2004.htm.
3. MARC records use fields in the 600s to provide information about subjects addressed by the item's content. The 655 field reports the item's genre, not in the critical sense but rather in the sense of identifying the work as an example of a type or as an instance of the format. Thus, some catalogers designate audiobooks or graphic novels as such on this tag.
4. B. M. Westby, *Sears List of Subject Headings* (New York: H. W. Wilson, 2004), is used by many school and smaller public libraries. The Library of Congress Office for Subject Cataloging Policy's *Library of Congress Subject Headings* is published both in print and online.
5. See appendix B for some of these titles.

CHAPTER 6

How Does the Collection Find New Readers?

Marketing and Promotion

Whether your library has been collecting and circulating graphic novels for some time or is just getting started with a graphic novel collection, it is important to reach out to potential graphic novel readers as well as to any established audience. This is true with any library collection, of course. The library needs to alert its target audience to the various formats it has to offer, explain why it offers them, and emphasize that it is open to considering suggestions for new materials.

When it comes to graphic novels, the library may encounter either spoken or unspoken prejudice among both library users and staff. Rather than sweeping the nascent collection onto a back shelf where it can be found only by devotees, it is healthier for all—the library and the public— to work on neutralizing prejudice through education.

PUBLIC PREJUDICES

At this point in American cultural history, graphic novel readers are relatively few in number. Although such readers range in age from baby boomers to children aged to but a single digit, more library users and potential users have read about graphic novels than have actually read a graphic novel. Due to some community members' lack of familiarity, your library's graphic novel collection may be the target of such prejudicial remarks as

> "Comic books aren't really literature and don't belong in the library, a temple of our intellectual elitism."

> "Graphic novels are just fancy comic books and comic books are only for kids. Put them in the children's section if you must make them available."

> "Graphic novels must be pretty raunchy. Consider the term *graphic*; I know what that means! So keep graphic novels away from kids who visit the library."

If you are getting wind of such outspoken prejudices, you are far ahead of libraries where such criticisms go unspoken and are thus less likely to be effectively addressed. And just because you are not hearing such remarks, you cannot assume that your community is completely behind your efforts to maintain a graphic novel collection. Many people outside the library, bookstore, and publishing communities do not fully understand that intellectual freedom always entails living with ideas or aesthetics that can be personally offensive. Consequently your dialogue with the community will be more productive if you focus on educating instead of arguing.

Demonstrate the Fallacies of the Prejudices

Instead of verbally countering negative assertions, provide ready access to materials and information that show exactly why the stated prejudices are not the end of the argument. There are, indeed, literary graphic novels for a variety of reading tastes. Placing them on genre lists among the titles of traditional books with similar themes orients library users to the relevance of titles in the graphic novel format.[1] Physical displays that include graphic novels among materials in more traditional formats will also demonstrate to the public that many kinds of publications share qualities that transcend format.

Responding to the notion that graphic novels are merely fancy comic books requires you to be judicious. Certainly, tossing a tale by R. Crumb among the picture books is not a useful approach if you really hope to win support for your cause of collecting graphic novels![2] On the other hand, Harvey Pekar has done much to clarify how and why there is an adult audience for graphic novels: kids are not interested in prostate cancer, but many a middle-aged person has found and will continue to find comfort and insight in Pekar's examination of his own experience with that disease.[3]

And even though people in libraries and publishing may have agreed on the meaning of *graphic novel*, there is no reason to assume that the general public has ever heard that term in reference to a book that appears to have—and really does have—many visual traits in common with a comic book pamphlet. We certainly use the term *graphic* in a very different sense when describing why some movies are given a rating of Restricted by the Motion Picture Association of America's movie rating board. Does everyone in your community refer to mass market paperbacks as such? Any chance that such nomenclature could lead some people to jump to inaccurate—albeit interesting—assumptions about content?

To avoid possible misapprehensions, libraries generally use signage that employs the most common names for various formats: videos, paperbacks, comic books. They might not be the bibliographic terms of choice, but they do let nonspecialists know what we have. Posting redundant or bibliographically "impure" signs, such as "Comic Books and Graphic Novels," allows the uninitiated to draw more accurate conclusions about what a new term might mean.

Speak Up

Seek and accept invitations to address the local media about the library's graphic novel collection(s). Libraries are granted opportunities to present public service announcements about relevant programming, large gifts, and popular new formats. Include information about the library's graphic novels in the spokesperson's comments.

In addition, note the library's graphic novel collection when you speak to other agencies. Present public programs about graphic novels, and be sure to promote both the relevant collection and the program.[4] For example:

> When publicizing a cartooning workshop, mention the library's graphic novel collection, where it is located, and whom it is designed to serve.
>
> Include titles of graphic novels when working with teachers or others who turn to you for assistance in curriculum planning.
>
> When asked by local book clubs to make title suggestions, include graphic novels and explain why each would be a suitable candidate for the groups to consider discussing.

Neutralizing Prejudices

By treating graphic novels with the same respect and authority granted to other formats, library staff can do much to attract new readers to graphic novels. Certainly not every library user—or potential library user—has the visual orientation that makes graphic novel reading enjoyable. However, by asking questions about format preferences during readers' advisory interviews and listing graphic novels among the choices to fulfill a subject or genre request, the library opens access to the graphic novel collection to people who may be unaware of the format or of their own possible interest in it.

Allowing the graphic novel collection—or the mass market paperback collection, for that matter—to become visibly worn and shabby sends the public a clear message that the library lacks respect for that format. The graphic novel collection should be weeded for condition as thoroughly as any other collection if the public is to see that its contents matter.

CROSS-MARKETING FORMATS

Shelving and readers' advisory work are two bibliographic methods that can be used to market graphic novel collections.

Shelving Options

Shelving can be used in a number of ways to cross-market graphic novels. For example:

> Intershelving graphic novels with traditional print sources, especially when the library owns few graphic novels, firmly suggests to users that the graphic novel is a legitimate part of the library's offerings on a topic.
>
> Providing easily visible and accessible shelving space for graphic novels allows library users to see that such materials exist at the library and that they warrant a prime location.
>
> Shelving graphic novels face out gives library users the opportunity to judge the books by their covers and to note that such judgments are more wisely used with graphic novels than with traditional books.
>
> Shelving all formats together—traditional print, audiobooks, graphic novels, feature and documentary films—suggests to library

users that the many formats for presenting information or stories are of equal value and are equally available to them. However, because different formats require different types of equipment and access, shelving all formats together as a form of cross-marketing is best used in displays rather than throughout the library.

Readers' Advisory Work with Graphic Novels

Library staff who perform readers' advisory services on demand must be cognizant of all the possible tastes that service users may bring to them. It is not enough to have your own favorite ten titles to suggest. In fact, it is necessary to be fluent in a variety of genres, especially when readers' advisory questions are caught on the fly rather than by highly trained advisors placed at points close to a stockpile of advisory tools.

Including Graphic Novels with Other Format Suggestions

From a marketing perspective, the readers' advisor who includes a graphic novel title or two in every short list of reading suggestions is doing yeoman's work toward making the graphic novel collection visible and viable. Although it is pointless to suggest graphic novel titles to people who have clearly articulated that they have no interest in that format, almost any other advice seeker can be offered the opportunity to consider it.

Performing Readers' Advisory Work for Graphic Novel Lovers

Just as some readers' advisory seekers clearly want focused help in identifying material that will make them conversant with life in Victorian London or audiobooks for a long car trip, some people specifically want suggestions about graphic novels. Assuming that the staff handling such an inquiry has some expertise in readers' advisory work in general and is familiar with at least some of the contents of the library's graphic novel collection, the following become key questions in the graphic novel readers' advisory interview:

> "Do you find yourself moving through most graphic novels that
> you have enjoyed by reading the text or following the

images?" Most graphic novel readers can answer this question readily, and their individual responses help clarify whether they are more visually inclined or more text oriented.

"Are you interested in a particular graphic novel style?" This question would follow up on a more general question about preferences for a particular genre or subject matter regardless of format. Responses help focus the advisor on whether to include titles from the *manga* collection, for instance, in the list of suggestions.

"What have you already found in our collection of graphic novels that you like a lot?" In addition to supplying information about what readers mean when they say, "I want another just like . . . ," the responses to this question can help the library to evaluate how well the current graphic novel collection serves the local audience.

SEEKING MARKETING GUIDANCE

When developing promotional plans for the library's graphic novel collection, look to retail as well as to library-oriented marketing ideas. If there is a local comics shop, ask its proprietors why they chose the particular shelving techniques you find there. Ask people who already use the library's graphic novel collection if they also shop or browse elsewhere for graphic novels. Visit the stores they mention and consider how the merchandise is presented.

Buying Multiple Copies

Retail stores regularly rely on visual redundancy when promoting a product. The effectiveness of that approach is often overlooked in library promotions. Because the library budget usually requires the selector to choose between multiple copies of a limited number of titles or single copies of more titles, it is important to consider what can be gained by buying multiple copies of some graphic novels.

For example, multiple copies are very useful in displays, where they can be arranged at a variety of angles, drawing browsers from different directions and highlighting various strong points of the content.

In addition, popular titles often accumulate lengthy waiting lists—and many frustrated reserve holders—if too few copies are available. Depending on the library, the opportunity to "vote" for more copies by placing a hold on a title that is checked out may not be an option. And very often, children do not place reserves if something they want is not immediately available. In such cases, there is even no way to measure how many copies might be needed unless you hear from library staff or users who are aware of specific failed attempts to retrieve popular titles.

Finally, at a time when some schools and teachers are aware that graphic novels can be useful in certain areas of study, it reinforces goodwill to have ample numbers of such curriculum-friendly materials on hand.

Supplying Sufficient Light

People typically browse graphic novels before deciding which ones to borrow or buy. Although good lighting should be available throughout the library, it is a necessity to the marketing of the graphic novel collection. To that end, the collection should be placed where there is sufficient light right at the shelf to ensure that readers will be comfortable when looking through the interiors of the materials. Marketing graphic novels in a dim corner carries a very real message—and it is not a positive one.

Posting Signs

Bookstores that stock graphic novels and comics often play on their visual richness by including images in pertinent signage. To broker an agreement among administrators about the relevance of such image-driven signs, you might find an ally in the children's library. If that territory, too, sports text-only signage, look back to the retail sector. How successful is the signage in a bookstore's picture book area? What contributes to the signs' success? How do images attract and steer store visitors who are looking for particular types of reading?

Too many signs and too many images in a small space confuse the onlooker. But a text-only signage policy shortchanges any library collection that includes formats that extend beyond text only.

Book Talking

Sharing information about and enthusiasm for specific titles through the public performance known as book talking offers some challenges to marketers of graphic novel collections. As with other readers' advisory work, book talking may include graphic novels among other formats, or it may focus on graphic novels alone. In either case, the book talker will need props to do good service to the graphic novels being featured.

MIXED-BAG BOOK TALKS

Including graphic novels among traditional text-oriented titles might seem like a natural choice if you are giving a book talk to an audience of middle or high school students. However, plan well or your presentation may feed into some kids' and teachers' false assumption that graphic novels are typically for youths and that youths are the only appropriate audience for graphic novels. If you plan to include just one or two graphic novels in a book talk for adolescents, make sure that your choices fit the theme or topic connecting the other books and that they clearly show the crucial role that images play in carrying the message.

Include a graphic novel or two or three when book talking adult audiences as well. There are plenty of titles that appeal to listeners with more life experience and broader aesthetic palates than most teens have developed. This, of course, is a perfect way to reach people who may know little or nothing about graphic novels but care about books, stories, and reading. It is also a perfect way to open the graphic novel collection to some uninitiated potential users and to discuss people's possible prejudices against the format. Obviously, any graphic novels you include must be worthy of the listeners' attention because by singling those titles out, you communicate that they are significant.

BOOK TALKS FEATURING GRAPHIC NOVELS ALONE

When your book talk will treat graphic novels only, it is wise to organize around a topic other than the format of the books. Keeping in mind that graphic novels represent a format, not a genre, and that successful book talking slates usually pull together titles that share a genre or subject, a book talk featuring graphic novels still requires the performer to address substantive commonalities among the titles selected.

Salting a book talk largely devoted to graphic novels with some titles in alternative formats helps to widen the audience's awareness of those formats as well. Among the relevant alternates are

a traditional print biography or autobiography of one of the graphic novelists whose work you are featuring;

a how-to book on drawing, cartooning, writing, or publishing;

a film about the work or life of one of the graphic novelists featured in your talk; and

recorded music from the place or period featured in one of the graphic novels you are book talking.

TIPS ON BOOK TALKING GRAPHIC NOVELS

Because no graphic novel can be reduced to words alone, it is necessary to plan how you will share both images and narrative content with your audience. Depending on the size of your audience and the page size of the graphic novel you plan to share, merely holding up a page spread may work. The page spreads that you display should be carefully chosen because their images must both represent the larger work and make sense to audience members who are not familiar with the story as a whole. Suitable page spreads are likely to

include a full-page image on one side and three or four panels on the facing page;

be rendered in a clear-line style; and

be printed at least folio sized.

Among the page spreads to avoid are those that

depict extreme violence, nudity, or illegal activities;

include so much activity that considerable study is necessary to understand the details;

give away plot resolution; or

contain images so small that that they cannot be seen from a distance.

Instead of relying on a page spread to give the audience a taste of the graphic novel's images, you may want to show the picture of just one character. This is most easily achieved by photocopying a page on which that character appears as clearly and as free of other intrusive lines as possible. Enlarge the copy so that it is of suitable size for the environment in which you are book talking. Because you are not going to distribute the photocopy or be duplicitous about the identity of the art's creator, your use of the copy within the book talk forum is fair.

In addition to displaying sample images, what else should you include when book talking graphic novels? As with any book talk, there is no single right answer. What to include depends on the book's overall content and your own personality, as well as on the nature of the audience. Certainly, simply showing images should never replace talking about at least one of the graphic novel's other attributes: plot, protagonist, theme, authority, or authorship. In addition, the book talk should tie together all works mentioned through references to each one's organization, reading level, and suitability for the audience.

As a courtesy to your coworkers, be sure to provide a list of what you book talk at the library or libraries most likely to be visited by your audience. Audience members may accuse the library of bait and switch if they hear about a graphic novel at your book talk, visit the library to find it or something like it, and cannot find anyone who recognizes what they are describing.

PROGRAMMING AS MARKETING AND PROMOTION

Formal and ongoing programming provides continuous marketing and promotion of the library's collections. In the next chapter, we'll discuss a variety of articulated program possibilities beyond book talks.

NOTES

1. See appendix B for a collection of themed lists of graphic novels.
2. Crumb's work includes that scion of Underground Comix, the substance-elevated and sexually ravenous Mr. Natural, and Fritz, a cat unlikely ever to be confused with the one imagined by Dr. Seuss.
3. Joyce Brabner and Harvey Pekar, *Our Cancer Year* (New York: Four Walls, Eight Windows, 1994).
4. Programming with graphic novels will be discussed in detail in chapter 7.

How Can You Put Legs on Your Graphic Novels?

Creating Programs to Get the Collection Up and Walking

The contemporary library serves as a community programming resource as well as a repository for collections. Whether your graphic novel collection is part of a library that serves a school, a private club, or the general public, you can design programs that expand the community's awareness of graphic novels and the potential that format holds for intellectual and aesthetic exploration.

Ideally, library programming is part of an organic whole that addresses local needs, builds on collection strengths, and capitalizes on staff interests. Programming with graphic novels adds a dynamic element to the collection by taking the materials off the shelf and making them a focus of activity.

WHAT AUDIENCE DO YOU WANT TO REACH THROUGH PROGRAMMING?

In a library where graphic novels exist for several different demographic groups, programs related to graphic novels should be targeted to one of those specific groups. Such attempts at outreach are no different from programs related to the general book collections that are aimed at appropriately defined groups. However, in libraries where the graphic novel collection has been tied to a specific age-group or other definable group (for instance, browsers in a library where the graphic novels are uncataloged), potential graphic novel users will be frustrated if programming efforts fail to match that audience.

Several years ago, *Yu-Gi Oh!* tournaments became a moderately popular form of programming for older children.[1] Yet a library that stocks graphic novels only for adults, and thus has neither *Yu-Gi Oh!* nor other juvenile titles, would be sending a mixed and frustrating message to both children and adults if it tried to offer such a tournament. Another example of poor programming would be the screening of *anime* films suited to older teens and adults in a library where graphic novels are available only in the children's collection. When the program audience and the collection audience are mismatched, programs do not support the collections and collection users feel cut off from programming efforts.

Happily, the graphic novel format easily lends itself to programming that crosses demographic lines. There are *anime* films that resonate with highly diverse audiences, just as there are guest speakers who may be popular with a range of demographic groups. But intergenerational and other mixed-group programs need to be planned carefully if they are to be done well. The nature of a program's intended audience affects the day and time of its scheduling, shapes the means and style of its publicity, and guides the presenters in preparing content. Understanding whom you are trying to reach is essential to a program's ultimate success. A few of the groups who can profit from graphic novel programming are

- school-age children in general
- teenagers in general
- middle school girls
- literate adults
- young men
- college students
- art students
- journalism students
- adult literacy students
- teachers
- library staff

- English-language learners
- film buffs

Consider the decisions that have been made about housing and accessing the graphic novel collections you have built. Are those decisions compatible with the audience you want to reach through programming related to the graphic novel collection?

AUTHOR AND ARTIST PRESENTATIONS

Not every community can boast its own published graphic novelist, but any library with an active web presence can offer its audience online presentations by well-known graphic novelists. Using your web page as both a programming and a promotional tool expands your resources for expert presentations. In addition to promoting the library's graphic novel collection, such an online presentation notifies local talent of the library's interest in promoting their art and of the potential local audience for that art. So, while planning an on-site program, offer your community peeks inside the works and interviews with luminaries of the world of graphic novels. See appendix A for websites offering such material.

The Graphic Novelist as Performer

Hosting a creator of graphic novels carries the same responsibilities as hosting an author or illustrator of any other type of book. In addition to alerting the appropriate target audience to the artist's scheduled appearance, an honorarium must be offered, space made available, and so on. Follow the same protocol you use when hosting a narrative biographer or a picture book illustrator:

Research a potential speaker's history as a presenter. Can she speak as well as she creates graphic novels? Which other audiences have enjoyed her presentations, and how closely do they resemble your target audience? Make the arrangements well in advance to allow for sufficient publicity.

Discuss fees and be prepared with a check on the day of the presentation.

Make sure that the presenter has a place to stash personal items, knows where to take care of creature comforts, and has space to move around comfortably while speaking with the audience.

Verify in advance what technology will be needed to ensure a successful program. For example, does the presenter have slides to show? Is the setting appropriate for the size and distribution of the expected audience?

Be sure that you and the presenter understand each other's position on selling materials in conjunction with the program. Because many graphic novelists work with small presses or self-publish, they usually welcome every opportunity to sell their works to a receptive public. If your library proscribes such activities, let the presenter know that during your initial discussions. If, on the other hand, presenters are allowed to sell their materials in your library, be sure to arrange an appropriate area for sales after the presentation.

Where can you find a graphic novelist willing to present a program? If you have a local comics shop, or if a local bookstore carries a good selection of graphic novels aimed at the same demographic you hope to attract to your program, discuss the options with the proprietor or manager. If no such businesses exist in your community, you may want to invite a graphic novelist whose work is pertinent and likely to appeal to your target audience. Of course, if you hope to bring in a presenter who lives outside your area, you may need to pay sizable travel and accommodation costs in addition to an honorarium large enough to make the trip worthwhile.

Most graphic novelists lack the income to hire agents, so you will need to take other approaches to finding a graphic novelist for your program. Try the following:

> Contact the publisher of a graphic novelist's most recent work and explain that you want to invite the creator to participate in a library program.
>
> Contact the publisher of graphic novels that your community particularly enjoys and ask for suggestions about creators to invite. If travel money is short, say so. Then the publisher can limit the suggestions to people who may, in fact, be relatively nearby, or the publisher may be able to help fund the artist's trip as a promotional effort. Do not expect graphic novel publishers to have funds for promotion, however. Most of them run on slim margins.
>
> Discuss your search with arts-related agencies, including the local arts council, if you have one in your community, and high school or community college art teachers. Not only are you

highly likely to get leads on possible presenters, but you will also be networking with exactly the collaborators you need to contribute to the program and promote it.

After you have arranged for a graphic novelist to make a presentation at your library, make sure that your collection contains a sufficient number of the creator's books to meet the demand that the program will most likely generate. If the presenter's work is not yet included in the collection, you certainly need to add some titles before program day—and that means not just purchasing them, but also ensuring that they are processed and available for readers by the day of the program.

Online Programming with a Graphic Novelist

One way to prime your audience for the program is to use the library's home page to direct them to the presenter's website or online interviews. Those who work in the graphic novel format are usually computer-savvy and frequently use the Internet to build their own community. Often, their publishers feature pages from their books online, another resource toward which to point your audience from your library's home page.

ART AND PUBLISHING PROGRAMS

Because graphic novels are a form of sequential art, programs connecting your collection to related media offer natural opportunities to promote it. Such programs work best if the audience is limited to people sharing similar interests, skill levels, or ages. The similarities will help the program leader to keep everyone engaged and on task.

Cartooning Workshops

One option is to seek a professional cartoonist in the community to present a program on how to draw cartoons. Alternatively, if you would like to take the lead in such a program, there is an abundance of published materials that can help you teach yourself some cartooning.

The content of cartooning workshops can be adjusted to fit the target audience. It is feasible to conduct them as a series, with each session building on skills and knowledge gained in the previous session. A cartooning workshop may also be presented as a single session targeted to a specific group.

It is crucial to keep a specific group in mind as you plan a cartooning workshop. Those who attend will come with a variety of skill levels, so it is best not to complicate the situation by permitting too many other differences. For example, mixing proficient middle school cartoonists with curious but relatively circumspect senior citizens may make everyone feel uncomfortable, unless you have a very skillful presenter. Demanding too much or too little of participants should also be avoided. People are much more likely to attend subsequent programs if they feel that their first program entertained them or taught them something worthwhile.

Again, use your library's website to support your series of cartooning workshops. If participants grant permission, you can mount their work in an online gallery, either at the end of the series or throughout to show how particular pieces progress.

SPECIAL POPULATIONS

Cartooning workshops may be appealing to some of the special users of your library. Consider the potential for such a program targeting the participants in your adult literacy project, or for another program targeting English-language learners. However, with both groups, be sensitive to the fact that comics are not naturally easier to read for people with literacy or language access issues. Graphic novels require readers to work with text and to understand cultural references depicted in images. Making their own cartoons, however, places literacy or language students in the driver's seat—what they produce they can read.

ZINES

One development that has brought more women into the comics field was the rise, in the early 1990s, of zines. Because zines are self-published, they gave women more opportunities to get into print without having to rely on male-dominated publishing houses. They also allowed women to escape the pressures to conform to those male-dominated publishers' concepts of what is interesting. Zines, whether serials or single issues, continue to be produced and distributed informally by leaving stacks of them on the freebie or give-away shelves of libraries, music stores, and bookstores, or by posting them online or on community bulletin boards like those found in Laundromats and supermarkets. Zines can be produced by anyone with a yen to write or draw and enough money to photocopy the results in quantity for such grassroots distribution.[2]

But what do zines have to do with graphic novel programming? Some zines are themselves graphic novels or contain comic strip series. Beyond that, there often is cross-over appeal among zine creators for graphic novels. Organizing an opportunity to share zines, or to create zines, is another way to alert your public to your library's efforts to collect graphic novels.

BOOK DISCUSSIONS OF GRAPHIC NOVELS

Nonfiction works in graphic novel format are excellent candidates for book discussion groups.[3] Frequently, the graphic novel format presents nonfiction subjects—war, imprisonment, grave sickness—so powerfully that discussion may be *demanded* in order for individual readers to digest the content intellectually or emotionally. Fictional graphic novels may also be good candidates for discussion, of course.

As with any other programming, the target group must be clarified before a particular title is chosen to discuss. Will the discussion be a one-time event, the occasion of a "One Community, One Book" type of effort? Or will the discussion group—whether children, teens, or adults—meet regularly and view graphic novels as just one of several types of books to be considered? Or will the discussion group meet regularly and be devoted solely to graphic novels? In the last case, the group may include members of many different ages, drawn together by interest in the format, and you may have to choose titles carefully in order to keep everyone in the group suitably challenged.

When members of a discussion group will be exposed to only a single graphic novel (within the context of the group, at least), there is room to compare and contrast that format with text-driven books, films, and other media. And when a discussion group will work its way through two or more graphic novels, you can compare and contrast works within the same format. Most people who would join a book group devoted exclusively to graphic novels are likely to have realms of knowledge and fields of discourse that extend well beyond the graphic novels read within the group. Such a group's moderator, then, must be truly well read and conversant in the field of graphic novels.

Choosing a Graphic Novel to Discuss

For groups that will discuss only a single graphic novel, consider the following when selecting a title:

themes of other books members have read within and outside the
group;

reading abilities and intellectual interests of group members;

availability to the group of information about the work's author
or artist;

production quality of the work, including clarity of printing; and

relevance of the work's subject or theme to members of the group.

The same factors should be considered when designing a list of titles
for a discussion group that will focus on graphic novels. However, two
additional concerns arise: the diversity of subjects or themes and the availability of other titles by authors featured in the discussions (through the
library's collections, of course!).

Conducting the Discussion of a Graphic Novel

Moderating the discussion of a graphic novel has much in common with
conducting any other kind of book discussion. Both discussions will be
geared toward eliciting remarks about how well the work communicates
its message. Both groups also will discuss features that seem to promote
or detract from enjoyment of the work and any understanding of life experiences the work enhances. But when discussing a graphic novel, the following questions also may be useful:

Was there some thematic use of a color, shading, background
image, or other pictorial element?

How successful was the creator in communicating his or her attitude toward the events presented? Was attitude communicated textually or through image and perspective?

How did this work's treatment of the topic compare with text-
only material you have read on the same, or a similar, subject?
Was this treatment more or less informative than others? To
what do you attribute the differences in your perception of the
subject as presented here and as presented in other types of
publications?

What were you left to envision for yourself because it neither
appeared in images nor was fully described in words? How
was that an appropriate or a difficult kind of blank for your
mind's eye to fill?

What style of art appeals most to you in the books we have read in this discussion group? Does that style seem to suit a particular type of story?

The California Center for the Book has packaged a graphic novel discussion program that warrants emulation and variation by similar agencies. It was designed for teen readers as its exclusive target group. Each of the eight or nine titles included in the package is accompanied by more than a dozen questions that invite discussion. Publishers, too, occasionally offer discussion questions to institutions to promote the purchase of some graphic novels. As in any book group, it may be most productive to limit the discussion to only two or three questions. Having many questions to choose among, however, enables the discussion leader to salvage or redirect discussions when participants seem hesitant or a single member dominates the floor.

GENERATE LOCAL REVIEWS OF GRAPHIC NOVELS

Young fans of graphic novels or comics series regularly attempt to emulate the artwork in their favorite books. By inviting young users of your graphic novel collection to submit reviews of the material they have read, you can encourage them to create graphic novel–style book reviews. Graphic novels call out for criticism and analysis in their own unique format.

To celebrate your young readers' work and—not coincidentally—to draw more attention to the graphic novel collection, display the reviews where other library users can see them. You can mount them as shelf talkers near or in the collection or, for even more far-reaching effect, scan them for display online.

EXERCISES AND LESSON PLANS

Material published for teachers to use in art and literature classrooms can be adapted for use in library programs. The National Association of Comics Art Educators maintains a website that includes links to teaching resources created by members of the association.[4] Depending on the age and size of your target group, the exercises described there and at other curriculum-support sites may provide you with just the right inspiration, and certainly with enough direction, to design a library program.

Materials created by participants during such lesson-driven programs may even merit inclusion in the library's permanent collection. Certainly the cataloging and circulating of materials created at the library encourage the creators—and their friends and families—to visit the library and explore other available resources.

Pedagogical sources sometimes list graphic novels by theme.[5] This is useful for programmers who must design several types of programs, or programs for different types of audiences. Some of the library's holdings may be appropriate for one audience while other holdings may work more successfully with another audience. An exercise may be suitable for one group while a list of graphic novels related to that exercise may be helpful in mounting a display that reaches other groups.

ELEMENTS OF GRAPHIC NOVELS IN OTHER PROGRAMMING

Readathons and programs that incorporate such elements as costumes, photo opportunities with celebrities, images of celebrities, or films may lend themselves to offshoots that relate to graphic novels. These are great ways to introduce graphic novels to a wider audience, particularly in libraries where the collection is familiar to only a small group. Begin by explaining what graphic novels are and why specific titles are mentioned in the general program.

Graphic Novels and Film

American movie companies regularly offer feature films depicting the adventures of comic book heroes, but the Japanese art form of *anime* is even more closely linked to *manga*. Unlike the filmed, live-action versions of Superman and Spider-Man, *anime* films may be of any length. A short one may be incorporated into a book group's discussion of the animator's print work, while feature-length ones may be included in an ongoing film series intended to expose the audience to a variety of cinematic styles.

Some American films, such as *Ghost World* or *American Splendor*, have obvious links to the graphic novel collection.[6] Of course, when planning to present any film to a group be sure to acquire appropriate public performance rights.

Graphic Novels Supporting Other Programs

A graphic novelist, a book discussion about a graphic novel, or an *anime* film may be the perfect adjunct to a library program planned to address another topic altogether. For instance, you can enhance a program about bullying with a graphic novel that addresses the same theme. Or, if your program deals with sexual orientation, invite a graphic novelist who has written about that theme to speak to the group.[7]

KEEPING UP THE COLLECTION

Successful programming should bring new users' attention to your graphic novel collection. As interest grows, you may need to reevaluate the collection's size, scope, and placement. Analyze the feedback you gather from program participants who subsequently use the collection to revise what you know about your library's users and their needs and how those factors affect the graphic novel collection.

Be sure to communicate the changes you think are needed to appropriate staff and administration, using the data gathered from your program attendees to explain why your suggested changes would better serve the public.

Selection, accessibility, and promotion are relevant to all formats in your library's collection. Graphic novels may be unique, however, in terms of the political aspects entailed in their upkeep. In the final chapter, we focus directly on issues of intellectual freedom, popular culture, and resources beyond the library community that can assist your efforts on behalf of the graphic novel collection.

NOTES

1. One of several trading card games that appeal to elementary school fans, as well as to older players who organize full-fledged tournaments, this Japanese import also supports a recent Warner Brothers movie.
2. See Francesca Lia Block and Hillary Carlip, *Zine Scene* (Los Angeles: Girl Press, 1998), for extensive information about the history and social science of zine publishing.
3. See appendix B for a list of nonfiction graphic novels.

4. The National Association of Comics Art Educators' suggested links to teaching resources can be found at http://www.teachingcomics.org/resources.php.
5. Ibid.
6. Daniel Clowes wrote both the graphic novel *Ghost World* and the live-action film based on it (Seattle, WA: Fantagraphics Books, 1997; Santa Monica, CA: MGM, 2000). The film *American Splendor* (Burbank, CA: HBO, 2003) explores the comic book publishing world, a close relative of the graphic novel publishing culture. Both films are rated R by the MPAA.
7. See appendix A for websites that offer information about graphic novels that treat topical issues.

CHAPTER 8

The Politics
of Graphic Novels

History has demonstrated that reading can be seen as a subversive activity, and that some categories of reading are perceived popularly and theoretically as potentially more subversive than others. Fifty years after Dr. Wertham's cold-water bath treatment of comics, as discussed in chapter 1, our culture still attributes an edgy identity to sequential art–based books. It is certainly not the first—or even the most recent—format to be scrutinized and found suspect by multiple segments of the cultural continuum. And, in fact, graphic novels are themselves a part of that continuum, expressing best what other formats can express less well, but certainly not vying to replace other media and their variety of superior uses.

INTELLECTUAL FREEDOM

The less effectively any expressive art is integrated into popular acceptance and perception, the more its legitimacy is likely to be challenged. Only rarely are best sellers in the adult book market challenged by censors, but literary works taught in schools more frequently attract such attention. What is perceived as mainstream on some European newsstands might well be identified as pornographic by many Americans. In households where both adults and children play electronic games, the age appropriateness of a particular game will be judged differently than in households where adults see only discrete moments of electronic games. While we judge what we know, we can be even quicker to judge things that we know little about. When published expressions are seen out of context by people who are unfamiliar with their format, they are liable to be misjudged.

Typical Challenges

Graphic novels present readers not only with ideas—as do text-only works—but also with images. The graphic novel *reader* makes use of both, but the graphic novel *viewer* typically leafs to one page or another, scans the images, and, perhaps, takes in one or two passages of text. Because the viewer disassociates the parts from their whole, he or she is more likely to complain about

- depictions of or attention drawn to violence
- depictions or discussions of sexuality
- disrespect for women
- disrespect for adults
- disrespect for persons of authority
- ease of access by children
- crass treatment of a subject demanding sensitivity

Concerned parents and other adult guardians are likely to publicly challenge a specific graphic novel in a library's collection. However, library staff are more likely to generalize their personal distaste for a few items they have seen casually and incompletely into a negative attitude toward the format as a whole, which they may communicate either passively or actively. Passive behaviors, such as grumbling about the money the library is "wasting" on the purchase of graphic novels, may damage morale, but more active protests, such as "losing" material that is to be processed or shelved, damages the collection, the users, and the library's budget as well. Listen to staff grumblings and address them expeditiously, knowing that such perceptions may be shared by some part of the library's public. You need an educated and cohesive workforce if you are to rise to challenges that are more demanding than expressions of discontent.

Policy Education

Be sure that the library staff understands that collection policies are maintained across the board. Staff members who want to challenge specific items in the collection must abide by the same procedures as the public. To do so, they must have both access to and understanding of those procedures. The topic of intellectual freedom should be covered when new staff members are trained and oriented in your library and in regular staff-development programs thereafter. In such settings, questions about collection development and the procedures for reconsidering material in the collection can be addressed outside the strictures of a formal challenge.

Care with reviewing, selecting, placing, and promoting the graphic novel collection should ensure that any challenge to an item will be both taken seriously *and* limited to that specific item. It makes no more sense to view a challenge to a specific title as a critique of the entire graphic novel collection than it does to question the entire children's fiction collection because one library user (or staff member) objected to the art in a single picture book. Challenges must be specific in terms of both the title and the grounds for complaint.

Meeting a Challenge

If and when a graphic novel in your collection is challenged, follow the steps you would for a challenge to any other material. Your collection development policy should provide directions for accepting and responding to a challenge.[1] The procedure should include

> clarifying with the challenger that he or she has read the work in its entirety and would like to make a formal complaint;
>
> having the challenger complete a formal, written request for reconsideration of the title;
>
> referring the recommendation for reconsideration both to the library's director, or lead administrator, and to the developer responsible for the collection in which the offending material is maintained;
>
> reviewing the challenged work directly by rereading it in light of the collection development policy and the challenge, and by finding and reading published reviews of the work;
>
> determining an appropriate response in light of the information that you have collected and analyzed;

communicating that response to the challenger; and

following through on the response by either maintaining the material where it was or moving it to a place that you now deem more appropriate.

There will, indeed, come a time when a challenger makes a salient point about the suitability of a particular work, graphic novel or otherwise, for its current place in the collection. Your library must be prepared to follow its own policies on reconsideration and to make an informed judgment that may differ from the judgment made when the material was first brought into the collection. Reconsideration must be informed rather than reactive. If the material would be better placed in an alternative location in the library—due to changes in the community's demographics, the size and scope of the graphic novel collection, or a combination of factors—move it because that is the right thing to do, not because a challenger told you to. By the same token, do not automatically refuse to make the change because you believe that the library should never admit that a challenger was correct.

There are many examples of libraries that made questionable or illegitimate responses to challenges to their graphic novel collections.[2] Avoid the intellectual dishonesty of errors like the following:

excluding graphic novels from your library's display of new materials to avoid calling attention to other titles already in the collection

placing all graphic novels, regardless of audience, in a restricted or specially monitored area of the library

withdrawing a graphic novel that has been challenged without completing the formal steps for reconsideration

moving a contested graphic novel from the collection in which it was challenged to a different collection where it does not fit (that is, the alternative location does not serve the users for whom the graphic novel is maintained in the collection)

requiring special review of *all* materials in the graphic novel collection, including all future acquisitions, because one title was challenged

responding to a challenge without rigor, dismissing the challenger as uninformed about graphic novels and thus unqualified to make the challenge

With proper planning and appropriate policies in place, the graphic novel collection *as a whole* should be no more susceptible to challenges than are other collections. If the collection as a whole is called into question, mistakes have been made in planning and promoting it. Such a challenge, if made formally, may require you to plan anew, making sure that knowledge about your community and about the graphic novels that you can make available guide both your collection development and your promotion of the collection.

THE COMIC BOOK LEGAL DEFENSE FUND

Libraries and communities facing challenges to their materials can find expert assistance through the American Library Association's Freedom to Read Foundation, its Office of Intellectual Freedom, or the American Civil Liberties Union. When the challenged material is a comic book or graphic novel, another resource is the Comic Book Legal Defense Fund (CBLDF). This nonprofit organization works on several legal fronts where comics, cartoonists, and access issues are concerned.

The Comic Book Legal Defense Fund is an organization in need of support by people who value access, through libraries and otherwise, to graphic novels. Rather than waiting for your own difficulty to arise, become acquainted with the issues as the CBLDF publicizes them.[3]

Among the concerns the CBLDF works to mediate are disparities between intellectual property laws pertaining to cartoonists and those pertaining to mainstream authors. Intellectual freedom begins long before a reader gains access to a book; whether a publisher can acquire a work to publish is an issue of intellectual freedom. Graphic novel publishers, readers, and writers all have interests in protecting intellectual freedom. This concern, given the disadvantages of the graphic novel's identity as an alternative form of expression rather than an integrated element of the cultural mainstream, is replete with economic and political implications specific to the format.

IMPLICATIONS OF GOING ALTERNATIVE

Although this book exists because libraries are moving a little closer to accepting graphic novels, the fact is that people in the graphic novel business—writers, artists, publishers, booksellers—are not, for the most part, getting rich from their efforts. They are working at an edge that most people continue to see as an alternative to the mainstream.

As a result, libraries must face some demographic and economic realities if they hope to make the best of collecting and promoting graphic novels. Those realities are liable to be modified, however, as both culture and law change. Although the same issues apply to any library collection, they are exacerbated by the alternative identity still worn by graphic novels. For example:

> When compared with your community as a whole, the demographics of those who already have a vested interest in graphic novels may be skewed in terms of gender and age. Does your collection reflect that skew or seek to broaden the base of interested users?

> Community members who find the graphic novel collection appealing may not have the same amount of political power as those who prefer other collections. How will you maintain the library's interest in serving the less powerful constituency?

> Most graphic novel titles do not stay in print for long, and maintaining a balanced collection requires considerable sleuthing due to the scarcity of timely reviews. How will you maintain the standards on which you plan your collection?

> Most creators working in the graphic novel field are not adequately paid. How can the library provide meaningful support, especially when looking to those creators to help promote the library's collection?

> Library administrators are highly likely to have theoretical information about graphic novels but much less likely to have personal experience with them. How will that influence policies that apply to the graphic novel collection?

If your library's mission includes taking responsibility for exposing your community to ideas and providing ideas that inform, educate, or entertain, there is a place for graphic novels in both the collections and the services you offer. Determining the best ways to include them, however, is not formulaic. Work with what you know, find out what you need to know, and keep going back to your community, to your colleagues, and to published resources (including newly emerging graphic novels and ones that are now considered classics) in order to revise your last best effort to match the format with your professional hopes and expectations of it.

FAD OR FOOTHOLD?

One of the key differences between graphic novels and eight-track tapes is that the latter was a technology while the former is an art. Unlike their near relatives—which include both comic books and traditional books, movies, and opera—graphic novels have not been on the scene long enough to be instantly recognized as such by most library staff and users. Of course, there are pockets around the nation where the graphic novel is fully accepted, both as a format and as a library holding, but they continue to be exceptions.

The dilemma is that it can be difficult to maintain a stance of openness to the future, a stance of waiting to see if the graphic novel will win cultural acceptance as an intellectual resource, without influencing the situation. It is not easy to keep funding a collection that many perceive as a mere fad. But neglecting to fund it destroys the opportunity to educate those who cannot afford to purchase graphic novels or who lack access to an alternative source of the published material. Depending on your community and your own interests in the graphic novel format, you may be influencing taste—and distaste!—as much as you are responding to perceived interest.

Although the popularity of the graphic novel as a format may ebb and flow, the formal integrity of the medium disproves that it is a fad. A fad is two-dimensional, unable to lift and carry diverse expressions. And by its very essence the graphic novel *is* a diversity of expressions.

Until very recently, graphic novels were shut out of the American classroom—and the school library—for being poor purveyors of curricular support. Today, many schools have acknowledged the purposes that specific graphic novels can serve in supporting specific curricula and the roles they can play in promoting literacy, art, and critical thinking. Some forward-thinking school libraries not only include graphic novels in their collections but also address graphic novels formally and specifically in their collection policies.

How, then, to strengthen and expand the format's foothold in libraries? Try the following:

Expand awareness of the format in diverse parts of your library and eschew efforts to corral a graphic novel collection within an area maintained for a limited user group.

Identify local subject headings that will enable readers of graphic novels and library staff to make better use of the collection through the catalog.

Cost out an appropriate budget for your library to spend on graphic novels and identify graphic novels as a line item in the materials budget.

Cross generational lines to talk about graphic novels with staff and when working with your library's community.

Discuss options for bibliographic control, readers' advisory work, collection development, and programming related to graphic novels with other libraries and through professional organizations, whether formal (state and national associations) or informal (electronic discussion lists).

Books have been around for a very long time and human expression for considerably longer. Yet we continue to seek best practices for working with them. When it comes to best practices for graphic novels in libraries, we are, indeed, in a neonatal phase. We have begun. And it is no time for complacency.

NOTES

1. See appendix C for sample collection policies.
2. See a list of such incidents cited in Francisca Goldsmith, "How Comics Are Banned," *Busted* 2 (Summer 2003): 16–17.
3. For more information, see the Comic Book Legal Defense Fund website at http://www.cbldf.org.

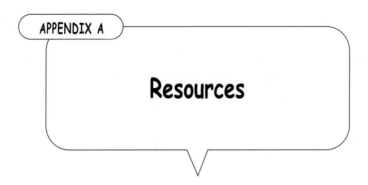

APPENDIX A

Resources

The resources listed here are intended to provide background material for those new to graphic novels and sequential art, and for those seeking assistance in identifying criticism, programs, and promotion leads related to graphic novels.

PRINT RESOURCES

Each of the titles below treats one or more facets of graphic novels, including their presence in libraries. Though some titles seem to apply to specific age-groups, their content may be adaptable to broader, or alternative, audiences.

Cary, Stephen. *Going Graphic: Comics at Work in the Multilingual Classroom*. Portsmouth, NH: Heinemann, 2004.

This specialist in second-language learning discusses both the research on and the practical applications of graphic storytelling to enhance English acquisition by students of all ages.

Eisner, Will. *Graphic Storytelling*. Tamarac, FL: Poorhouse Press, 1996.

How sequential art works in practical and aesthetic terms is addressed by the creator who is regularly credited with inventing the graphic novel format and name.

Gorman, Michele. *Getting Graphic! Using Graphic Novels to Promote Literacy with Preteens and Teens*. Worthington, OH: Linworth, 2003.

Aimed at those working with school audiences, this introduction to the format offers easy access to programming ideas.

Kneece, Mark, and Bob Pendarvis. *The Bristol Board Jungle*. New York: NBM, 2004.

Art school teachers worked with a college class to develop a graphic novel account of the making of comic book art.

McCloud, Scott. *Understanding Comics: The Invisible Art*. New York: Kitchen Sink Press, 1993.

In graphic novel format, this literary history traces the ancestry of the graphic novel and discusses the format's identifying characteristics.

———. *Reinventing Comics*. New York: Paradox Press, 2000.

As publishing moves into the computer age, McCloud updates his earlier critical work to reflect technology's influences in changing the production of comics.

Rothschild, D. Aviva. *Graphic Novels: A Bibliographic Guide to Book-Length Comics*. Englewood, CO: Libraries Unlimited, 1995.

More than four hundred titles are treated in evenhanded and insightful fashion, making this a stellar annotated bibliography for collection developers and book talkers.

Schodt, Frederik L. *Dreamland Japan: Writings on Modern Manga*. Berkeley, CA: Stone Bridge Press, 1996.

This history and critical guide to the development of *manga* is a good starting point for those new to the style.

Serchay, David S. "But Those Aren't Really Books! Graphic Novels and Comic Books." In *Thinking Outside the Book: Alternatives for Today's Teen Library Collections,* edited by C. Allen Nichols. Westport, CT: Libraries Unlimited, 2004.

This chapter addresses the specific collection needs of adolescents and reviews the all-ages issues of making collections accessible and maintaining their integrity.

Weiner, Stephen. *Faster than a Speeding Bullet: The Rise of the Graphic Novel*. New York: NBM, 2004.

This quick read is a good title to offer teachers who are new to the format.

ONLINE RESOURCES

Although some suggested sites may have links to commercial enterprises, they are all the independent creations of critics working with graphic novels and related publishing, and do not serve primarily as product outlets.

Brenner, Robin. No Flying, No Tights
http://www.noflyingnotights.com

Reviews and recommended lists are divided by age-group and address the interests and concerns of adult graphic novel readers, teen graphic novel readers, and children.

Ellis, Warren, and others. Artbomb
http://www.artbomb.net

Reviews and previews of graphic novels highlight those that are relatively sophisticated but accessible to readers with no memory of enjoying juvenile comics. The site also provides a portal to other substantive online comics sites.

Hahn, Joel. Comic Book Awards Almanac
http://users.rcn.com/aardy/comics/awards/

Local, national, and international awards include those that recognize graphic novel content and creation. This is a necessary and useful tool for researching.

Johnston, Antony, and others. Ninth Art
http://www.ninthart.com

Originating in the United Kingdom, this online weekly provides critical analysis in the form of reviews, interviews, and expository writing about comics publishing.

Lavin, Michael. Comic Books for Young Adults
http://ublib.buffalo.edu/libraries/units/lml/comics/pages/

Designed for a library school course at the State University of New York at Buffalo, this long-maintained site provides policy discussions, recommended book lists, and other information to assist the first-time graphic novel librarian.

Miller, Steve. GNLIB: Graphic Novels in Libraries
http://www.angelfire.com/comics/gnlib/index.html

Since 1999, GNLIB-L has provided an electronic discussion list on which library staff can discuss the plethora of issues related to graphic novels and comics in their diverse work-places. The home site provides list subscription information, archives, and collection development tools.

Poitras, Giles. The Librarian's Guide to *Anime* and *Manga*
http://koyagi.com/Libguide.html

Beyond definitions, recommendations, and directions to resources, this site offers discussions about differences between Japanese and American cultures, issues related to dubbing, and very specific considerations for library staff undertaking *manga* and *anime* collecting and programming.

Raiteri, Steve. Recommended Graphic Novels for Public Libraries
http://my.voyager.net/~sraiteri/graphicnovels.htm

Although subdivided into categories such as science fiction and comedy, many of the titles listed here are series with a fantasy or superhero inclination. The recommendations are thoughtful and include suggested age levels.

Sequential Tart
http://www.sequentialtart.com

Reviews and interviews spotlight the roles of women in the comics industry as creators, critics, and readers.

SMALL PUBLISHERS AND BIBLIOGRAPHIC SITES

These graphic novel publishers and bibliographers provide rich and deep online information about their books, their artists, and related topics.

Dark Horse Comics
http://libraries.darkhorse.com/reviews/firstlooks.php

Both single-volume works and new volumes in long-running series from this publisher are treated to profiles with accompanying full bibliographic data.

iComics
http://www.icomics.com

Sponsored by comicon, this site offers signed reviews of and artwork from graphic novels for all ages. There is direct access here to both Amazon and Mars Import for those who prefer to purchase their graphic novels from those commercial vendors.

Lambiek Comiclopedia
http://www.lambiek.net/artists/index.htm

Biographies and representative art by thousands of cartoonists, including those who write graphic novels and those who create *manga*, are easily searchable at this site maintained by a Dutch antiquarian comics shop.

Slave Labor Graphics
http://www.slavelabor.com/peepshow.html

Hot links to most of Slave Labor's titles include pages as well as press release information about each work's contents.

Tokyopop
http://tokyopop.com/manga.php

The *manga* publisher's many series are represented by artist and character information, sample images, and synopses of story lines.

Topshelf Productions
http://www.topshelfcomics.com

In addition to the publisher's graphic novel catalog, this site features reviews of new works and serves as a portal to interviews by its artists as they have aired and published in diverse media.

Viz Media
http://www.viz.com/products/backlist/

This *manga* importer and publisher has a handy search tool that will help collection or program planners locate Viz titles by genre.

Selected Graphic Novels By Category

The graphic novels listed here are arranged by broad category. The intent is to suggest starting points for those seeking suggestions for program ideas, readers' advisory work, curriculum connections, and book talking. Many booksellers, publishers, website keepers, librarians, and graphic novelists offer "Best of . . ." and "Top 10 . . ." (or 25 or 50) lists. Of course, all such lists become dated, especially if published on paper rather than online. The lists here are no less eccentric and personal than any other lists.

Titles in the lists vary in their suitability for various ages. If you are using this appendix as a selection tool, consider the appropriate audience at your library for each title. These lists are not "all ages," although a few of the titles may, indeed, work well with several ages in some communities and with different audiences in different communities.

With a format as new as the graphic novel, *classic* has to refer to something other than standing the test of time. Each of the listed works treats its theme well and exemplifies the format at its best both technically and creatively.

PEOPLE: REAL AND IMAGINARY

Brabner, Joyce, and Harvey Pekar. *Our Cancer Year*. New York: Four Walls Eight Windows, 1994.

Pekar and his wife put their experiences of living with his doctor's diagnosis of prostate cancer into a book, with artwork by Frank Stack.

Briggs, Raymond. *Ethel and Ernest*. New York: Knopf, 1999.

The author's parents, who provide the title and substance of this book, lived in Britain through two world wars, massive changes in technology, and campaigns by both economists and scientists to "educate" the working class.

Cruse, Howard. *Stuck Rubber Baby*. New York: Paradox Press, 1995.

A young, working-class white youth becomes engaged in the civil rights movement when his small Southern town reacts against it. In addition to identifying racism in his life for the first time, he also realizes his own identity as a gay man in a homophobic culture.

Eisner, Will. *To the Heart of the Storm*. New York: DC Comics, 2000.

The cartoonist credited with inventing the graphic novel explores his own family roots from the time of immigration to the United States at the turn of the twentieth century to his leave-taking on a troop train during World War II.

Gaiman, Neil, and Andy Kubert. *Marvel 1602*. New York: Marvel Comics, 2004.

The superhero pantheon of Marvel's publishing universe is transplanted to Elizabethan England by two master graphic novelists.

Hartman, Rachael. *Amy Unbounded: Belondweg Blossoming*. Wynnewood, PA: Pug House Press, 2002.

This cheerful little girl from the Middle Ages as they never were is both "safe" and entertaining for most ages.

9-11 Emergency Relief. Gainesville, FL: Alternative Comics, 2002.

Dozens of notable cartoonists and graphic novelists provide autobiographical stories of how they learned of and initially responded to the 2001 terrorist strike on the United States. Among the contributors to this effort to earn money for the Red Cross are Jessica Abel, Will Eisner, Harvey Pekar, Ted Rall, and Tony Millionaire.

Ottaviani, Jim. *Fallout: J. Robert Oppenheimer, Leo Szilard, and the Political Science of the Atomic Bomb*. Ann Arbor, MI: GT Labs, 2001.

The author has written several graphic novel–style nonfiction books about various scientists. This one explores how shared experiences do not necessarily make for shared perceptions of those events.

Rabagliati, Michel. *Paul Has a Summer Job*. Montreal: Drawn and Quarterly, 2003.

When he takes a last-minute offer of work at a summer camp, Paul discovers his own inner resources as well as an unrealized concern for children and an unexpected first love.

Tezuka, Osamu. *Buddha*. New York: Vertical 2003–.

The foremost Japanese cartoonist of the twentieth century created a sprawling history and exegesis of Siddhārtha Gautama, known as the Buddha, which will be complete in eight volumes in its English translation.

Winick, Judd. *Pedro and Me: Friendship, Loss, and What I Learned*. New York: Henry Holt, 2000.

After the two met on MTV's *Real World*, the titular AIDS educator inspired Winick so much that, as Pedro's health failed, Winick took up his activist work.

HISTORY, POLITICS, AND JOURNALISM

Anderson, Ho Che. *King*. Seattle: Fantagraphics, 2005.

Martin Luther King Jr.'s rise to leadership, the changing political landscape during the Johnson administration, and King's assassination and legacy are examined critically and in a variety of artistic techniques, including silhouette, collage, and vibrant color.

B., David. *Epileptic*. New York: Pantheon, 2005.

Although fictionalized, this account of how the author's family dealt with his older brother's epilepsy during the 1960s illuminates the growth of alternative lifestyle movements during that era, the prevailing memory of World War II in France, and the medical treatments for epilepsy that gained accept-ance—and sometimes rejection—during the period. The first part of this book was published under the same title by Fantagraphics in 2002.

Baru. *Road to America*. Montreal: Drawn and Quarterly, 2002.

Set during the Algerian war for independence from France, this story of a boxer's efforts to find a niche of personal fame in a time of political turmoil is told with colors and angles reminiscent of the 1950s.

Eisner, Will. *The Plot: The Secret Story of the Protocols of the Elders of Zion*. New York: Norton, 2005.

Eisner's posthumously published examination of the early twentieth century anti-Semitic fabrication shows the plot's first development and makes accessible how the lie became a propaganda reference point.

Geary, Rick. *The Borden Tragedy*. New York: NBM, 1997.

One of a series in which the author presents A Treasury of Victorian Murder, this recapitulation of the facts and theories surrounding the Fall River murders of Lizzie Borden's parents offers period perspective as well as analysis of the evidence.

Nakazawa, Keiji. *Barefoot Gen*. San Francisco: Last Gasp, 1990–2004, © 1987.

From the day the United States dropped the atom bomb on Hiroshima through the following week, how the citizens of the ruined city coped, sickened, died, and learned to live as orphans, scavengers, and the doomed is portrayed by the author, who lived it firsthand. First published in Japan in 1972.

Sacco, Joe. *Safe Area Goràzde*. Seattle: Fantagraphics, 2000.

The author is a cartoon journalist who reports from and about global hot spots wracked by ethnic and territorial dis-putes. Here he presents his interviews with and observations of the factions who lived and fought in and near the United Nations–designated demilitarized zone during the Bosnian war of the 1990s.

———. *Palestine.* Seattle: Fantagraphics, 2001.

The cartoon journalist reports on Palestinians' perceptions of Israel's encroachments on their homeland.

Satrapi, Marjane. *Persepolis: The Story of Childhood.* New York: Pantheon Books, 2003.

Born in Iran in time to witness its Islamic Revolution through the eyes of childhood, the author shows how such universals as family and home become particularized as much by the politics of the moment as by the culture that has developed in the place of her youth.

———. *Persepolis: The Story of a Return.* New York: Pantheon, 2004.

Satrapi's childhood ended with a more rebellious adolescence that took her outside her home country to the liberalizing influences of Europe. Upon her return home to Iran, she sees not only her culture with new eyes, but also her culpability as an individual aware of her own actions.

Shanower, Eric. *Age of Bronze: The Story of the Trojan War.* Orange, CA: Image, 2001–.

To date, two volumes, *A Thousand Ships* and *Sacrifice,* have been completed in this detailed and multilayered retelling of the Trojan War. Events on the various home fronts, the battles, and the politicized relationships between friends and across generations are realized in all their complexities.

Spiegelman, Art. *In the Shadow of No Towers.* New York: Pantheon, 2004.

The Pulitzer Prize–winning cartoonist offers his view and musings on the New York City left in the wake of September 11, 2001.

———. *Maus: A Survivor's Tale: My Father Bleeds History.* New York: Pantheon, 1986.

———. *Maus: A Survivor's Tale: And Here My Troubles Began.* New York: Pantheon, 1991.

The cartoonist tells his parents' story of surviving Auschwitz and goes on to examine his relationship with his father in later years.

LITERARY GRAPHIC NOVELS

Strong narrative and a developed use of symbolism and other literary devices inform the following titles.

Asamiya, Kia. *Batman: Child of Dreams*. New York: DC Comics, 2003.

Japanese cartoonist Asamiya places the American superhero in the role of protagonist in this tale about identity, the dangers of fame, and the false promises offered by pharmaceuticals.

Clowes, Daniel. *Ghost World*. Seattle: Fantagraphics, 1997.

Best girlfriends finish high school at a time when one is certain of what she wants her future to hold while the other needs more time—and patience—to identify herself as a young adult.

Deitch, Kim. *Boulevard of Broken Dreams*. New York: Pantheon, 2002.

The history and heartbreaks of animation's invention and eventual development into an industry inform the plot of this noir memoir.

Giardino, Vittorio. *A Jew in Communist Prague*. New York: NBM, 1997–.

The first three of its four volumes have been translated and published in the United States: *Loss of Innocence, Adolescence,* and *Rebellion*. The plot is revealed in the title and subtitles in a realistic novel about the anti-Semitism rife in postwar Eastern Europe and one young man's attempts to participate fully in a culture ruptured by maxims and countermaxims.

Hernandez, Gilbert. *Palomar: The Heartbreak Soup Stories*. Seattle: Fantagraphic Books, 2003.

Magic and realism wind together in these stories set in an imagined Central American community during a twenty-year period when powerful Luba—an iconographic and spirit-imbued woman—resides there.

Hosler, Jay. *Clan Apis*. Columbus, OH: Active Synapse, 2000.

The biological and social life of the honeybee is made into an engaging tale that offers both scientific accuracy and anthropomorphic insights on kinship, work, and the life cycle.

Kuper, Peter. *The Metamorphosis*. New York: Crown, 2003.

Franz Kafka's tale of the man who awakes to discover that he is now a cockroach is reconceived in visual format and retold from the viewpoint of the man's sister.

Llywelyn, Morgan, and Michael Scott. *Ireland: A Graphic History*. Rockport, MA: Element, 1995.

An episodic view of the dramatic history of the generations who have inhabited the Emerald Isle is stitched together with a love story and a raven.

Marvit, Lawrence. *Sparks: An Urban Fairytale*. San Jose, CA: SLG, 2002.

Her father is brutal and the guys she knows from her job at the garage fail to recognize her femininity, so this enterprising young woman builds herself the perfect boyfriend and stands up to Dad.

McCloud, Scott. *The New Adventures of Abraham Lincoln*. La Jolla, CA: Homage Comics, 1998.

Part sci-fi romp and part cutting political commentary on middle-class unconsciousness, a schoolboy hero saves the United States from space invaders who work their brainwashing trickery through the clever use of flag lapel pins.

Medley, Linda. *Castle Waiting: The Curse of Brambly Hedge*. Petaluma, CA: Olio, 2000.

Fractured Mother Goose tales come together in a robust and unified narrative that works all along the age spectrum.

Ott, Thomas. *Dead End*. Seattle: Fantagraphics, 2002.

Character, action, and plot, but no words, are featured in this pair of horror tales.

Pope, Paul. *Heavy Liquid*. New York: DC Comics/Vertigo, 2001.

In the near future, some hip young urbanites chase down a substance that can serve as both an artistic material for sculpting and an intoxicating drug.

Sen, Jai. *The Golden Vine*. Delhi, NY: Shoto Press, 2003.

Alternative histories work best when accurate history is relevant up to a point in the plot. The historical person of

Alexander the Great is at the heart of this gold-washed tale in which he collaborates with the Persians rather than overrunning them.

Sturm, James. *The Golem's Mighty Swing*. Montreal: Drawn and Quarterly, 2001.

In the days of the Negro Baseball Leagues, Jews, too, were relegated to the circuit.

Talbot, Bryan. *The Tale of One Bad Rat*. Milwaukie, OR: Dark Horse Comics, 1994.

Using a classic plot from young adult problem novels, the author explores how a young girl escapes her sexually abusive father and eventually finds new hope in a new home. Back matter shows how the graphic novel connects to other types of literature and how this graphic novel developed from ideas to images and words.

Thompson, Craig. *Good-bye, Chunky Rice*. Marietta, GA: Top Shelf Productions, 1999.

This tale of friendship, departure, adventure, and regret features a turtle, a mouse, a gruff but kind dock worker, a shady sea captain, and conjoined twins.

Collection Development Policies

Library collections containing graphic novels should be covered by development and evaluation policies that explicitly address that format. Such policies should include the following:

- Brief definition of the term to be used in the policy that allows for the broadest coverage of formats: *graphic novels, comics,* or another popularly recognized designation

- Explanation of where such items are maintained within the larger collection, whether as a part of each subcollection (adult, juvenile, etc.), or as a subcollection or an aspect of another special collection (such as a special art collection)

- Clarification of how titles are selected for inclusion in the collection

- Description of how the collection is regularly maintained and evaluated for condition, ongoing usefulness, and appropriate depth and breadth

- Directions for initiating reconsideration of particular contents in the collection

Collection development policies are to be used by library staff and published as a reference for the library's users. The collection development policy may exist, then, online or as a paper document. In either case, it must be readily available to all staff so that they can use it to respond to questions by library users and to guide the conduct of their own job duties.

SAMPLE STATEMENTS
OF COLLECTION POLICY

In collection development policies that address the scope and intentions of the collection in general terms, specific notes on formats may be appended to the general guidelines. In such cases, the graphic novel may be one of several specific format types noted, with only a few lines describing any qualitative issues relevant to collection development. Such a policy might say

> All materials in the collection should conform to the guidelines above. In addition, the following formats should include the attributes specified for them below . . .
>
> *Videos* . . .
>
> *Magazines* . . .
>
> *Graphic novels* should be selected for collections in which their content is age- and interest-appropriate. Both image and narrative should be noteworthy. Materials should be sound at the time of acquisition and repaired or replaced as they become worn.

Another approach would be to explicitly prescribe collection placement within the collection development policy:

> Graphic novels and other materials in comics format will be selected for inclusion in the adult fiction collection based on suitable published reviews. Other materials in those formats will be referred to the arts librarian for possible inclusion in the arts collection.

Or, instead of prescribing placement, the collection development policy may describe each subcollection by specifying which formats are to be included within it:

> The adult fiction collection contains books by American and foreign authors in English translation. Novels, short story collections, graphic novels, and mass market paperbacks are included in the adult fiction collection.

MODEL COLLECTION DEVELOPMENT POLICIES

The following is a brief list of libraries with collection development policies that include graphic novels and whose policies can be viewed in full on the Web.

Public Libraries

Campbell County (WY) Public Library System
http://www.ccpls.org/coldev/html/YA/xv-gn.html

Forsyth (IL) Public Library
http://www.forsythlibrary.lib.il.us/policy/4htm

Memorial Hall Library, Andover, MA
http://www.mhl.org/policies/cd/index.htm

Mercer County (NJ) Library
http://www.mcl.org/lib/colldev6.html

Morton Grove (IL) Public Library
http://www.webrary.org/inside/colldevadultya.html

State Library of Queensland (Australia)
http://slq.qld.gov.au/_data/assets/file/5863/coldevpol.doc

Tempe (AZ) Public Library
http://www.tempe.gov/library/admin/colldev.htm

School Libraries

James Solomon Russell Junior High School, Lawrenceville, VA
http://www.geocities.com/lisajunedenton/collection.html

Palmerston District Primary School, Northern Territory, Australia
http://www.palmdps.act.edu.au/resource_centre/policies/
collection_dvpt.htm

Sedro-Woolley (WA) School District
http://www.swsd.k12.wa.us/ct/lib/policy/coldev.htm

Academic Libraries

Brown University Library Collections: Visual Arts
http://www.brown.edu/Facilities/University_Library/collections/
colldev/subjects/visualart.html

Henry Field Library, Christchurch (New Zealand) College of Education
http://lib.cce.ac.nz/services/cdp.html

Michigan State University Special Collections Division: Comic Art
Collection
http://www.lib.msu.edu/comics/devpol.htm

INDEX

Francisca Goldsmith is the Collection Management and Promotion Librarian at Berkeley Public Library in California. She reviews a wide array of materials for a variety of professional journals and teaches staff development workshops in the areas of readers' advisory work, teen services, and working with graphic novels in a variety of library settings. She is an active member of ALA, YALSA, and several state and regional library associations. Across her twenty-five-year career, she has worked in academic and public libraries and on both coasts. She does not remember a comics-free period in her life.

Francisca Goldsmith is the Collection Management and Promotion Librarian at Berkeley Public Library in California. She reviews a wide array of materials for a variety of professional journals and teaches staff development workshops in the areas of readers' advisory work, teen services, and working with graphic novels in a variety of library settings. She is an active member of ALA, YALSA, and several state and regional library associations. Across her twenty-five-year career, she has worked in academic and public libraries and on both coasts. She does not remember a comics-free period in her life.